Healing The Broken Heart
A Messianic Mandate

David Levitt

Ammudim.org

Healing the Broken Heart book is copyrighted and may not be tampered with or copied for profit. Copyright 2025. First print 2025

Ammudim Teaching Ministries is a ministry of Congregation Ammudim. This material is owned fully and follows the copyright laws.

All Scripture references are from the King James Bible or the New King James Bible. Scripture taken is from the New King James Version©. Copyright © 1982 by Thomas Nelson. Used by permission. All rights reserved.

ISBN # 978-1-68026-119-6 first print 2025.

Ammudim®
TEACHING MINISTRIES
with David Levitt

Table of Contents

1. Identifying a Broken Heart. 9
2. A Messianic Mandate. 25
3. One War, Two Kingdoms. 45
4. The 'Pain' Of A Broken Heart. 79
5. Healing The Broken Heart From Reproach. 105
6. Healing The Broken Heart From Loss. 147
7. Closing Thoughts. 178
8. Prayers for a Broken Heart. 173
9. About The Author. 191

Before we begin, I would like to give a brief disclaimer on the terminology used in this book. You will quickly notice my use of the name Yeshua instead of Jesus. If you are unfamiliar with this name, Yeshua, it is the way to say Jesus in Hebrew. However, because of copyright laws, I have kept the name Jesus in the quoted Scriptures. Secondly, you will come across another term in this book called "the Body of Messiah". This is referring to the "church", but because of varying definitions and interpretations of the term "church" I have opted to us the term "Body of Messiah" which is referencing all those who make up the Body of believers in Yeshua for the forgiveness of sins through His atonement and the hope of the resurrection because of His resurrection.

Here is a quick reference guide:

Yeshua = Jesus
Messiah = Christ
Body of Messiah = Body of Christ / Church

Chapter 1

Identifying A Broken Heart

Identifying A Broken Heart

I want to begin our journey toward a whole and restored heart by asking you, the reader, three questions. After each question, I ask that you not go on to the next question but rather examine your life in the light of each question. Are you ready?

Question 1: Were you wounded by the words and/or actions of another, and since then, feel insecure and have difficulty trusting God and others? (Pause)

Question 2: Have you experienced a loss and gone beyond what would be considered "productive grief" into a perpetual absence of joy and meaning in life? (Pause)

Question 3: Are you a minister, pastor, counselor, or caring brother or sister trying to help someone who would have answered yes to the first two questions, but nothing, including prayer seems to be working when trying to help them? (Pause)

Identifying A Broken Heart

If you answered yes to one or more of these questions, it is a good indication that you are not just dealing with a psychological issue or negative emotions, but what the Bible calls a broken heart or a broken spirit. *(Please note I will use the terms a broken heart and a broken spirit interchangeably in this book.)*

Today, there are many misconceptions in our society as to what a broken heart really is and how it affects us. When most people think of a broken heart, images of broken romantic relationships, pop and country songs that talk of losing the guy or gal, or intense emotional responses to a loss are the things that most often come to mind. We may conclude these events hurt for a moment or even a while, but we often don't think of a broken heart as a spiritual issue, and not just a spiritual issue, but an issue that affects a person's entire life, including their physical health and relationships. Oh, and certainly men don't have broken hearts, just the ladies, right? Wrong! But think about it, even the term "broken heart" is feminized in our society and often relegated to an issue only women deal with or "weak" men. Maybe you have not thought of that but you know it's true. When was the last time you heard a man talking about a broken heart? I am going to let you in on something: crying and showing strong emotions (which is actually healthy, but men resist doing it) is not one of the requirements for identifying a broken heart. I believe that as we move on through this book, it will become clear that many men have broken hearts. You may know one of them, you may live with one of them, or you might be a man whose heart has been broken.

If that is you, take courage. Many men we read about in the Scriptures had broken hearts, and God healed them. In fact, some of the greatest men in the Bible knew the pain of a broken heart. Abraham, Moses, Job, Gideon, King David, and Jeremiah just to name a few. I too, have had a broken heart, and want you to know there is healing and God is able

Identifying A Broken Heart

to put us back together and use us mightily for His purposes in the earth.

I believe there is a disconnect in our understanding of a broken heart and how it can affect our daily lives. Here is what I mean, if someone says to us, "I have been dealing with some depression lately", is our first thought, "I wonder when their heart was broken?" Another person shares with you about a close friend or family member of theirs who is undergoing intense psychological or psychiatric therapy. Does the thought "I wonder who or what broke their heart" go through our mind? Please do not feel guilty or be hard on yourself if those thoughts are not there when you hear of these things. Most people have not truly been taught from the Scriptures, even in the Body of Messiah (more on that in the next chapter), the depths of how a broken heart can affect a person's life.

JUST HOW IMPORTANT IS OUR HEART TO OUR LIFE?

Let's take a look at the Proverbs.

Keep your heart with all diligence, For out of it [spring] the issues of life.
Proverbs 4:23 NKJV

Simply put, what this verse teaches us is that out of our hearts issues forth life. Who we are is on the inside, therefore guard it from things that would break it. Let's think about it. If our heart is broken then what can't issue forth? Life. When I say life can't issue forth, I am not speaking of mere existence, but life which has its substance in love, joy, peace, hope, and the like. If our heart is broken, life is not able to issue forth the way we desire it and in the absence of life, we have things that represent death like heaviness, anxiety, and despair. Of course, in this context, we are talking about the heart as the core of our inner man, our spirit, but if we observe how our physical heart works and serves us it is a great visual of what is happening spiritually.

WHAT DOES OUR PHYSICAL HEART DO?

I am not a medical doctor, but my basic understanding is that our heart is the organ responsible for pumping, or we could say sending blood to every other area of our body for its very survival. The blood that our physical heart pumps to different parts of our body carries with it oxygen, nutrients, hormones, and other key components necessary for those body parts to survive. It is common knowledge that if a part of our physical body has its blood supply cut off for a long enough time, that body part will actually experience tissue and molecular cell death. Basically, the body part dies because of the lack of blood flow, and depending on what body part is affected the entire body may die because other organs or functions that are essential for life may have died because the source of its life, the blood, was cut off. The Scriptures are clear, life is in the blood.

For the life of the flesh [is] in the blood: and I have given it to you upon the altar to make an atonement for your souls: for it [is] the blood [that] maketh an atonement for the soul.
Leviticus 17:11 KJV

Now we can go back to Proverbs 4:23 and see this more clearly from a spiritual perspective. If our heart, our spirit, is crushed and broken, life is not able to flow to other areas of our life, and our relationships, emotions, and even our physical bodies will not experience life and vitality the way God intended, but death. What the Bible calls a broken heart and the fruit that comes from a broken heart, the world often calls a mental illness. Could it be that problems that have a psychological label such as depression, anxiety, mania, schizophrenia, PTSD, and the like could have a broken heart at the core of the issue? I will tell you from experience that a broken heart is not the issue 100% of the time, but it is MOST of the time in these diagnoses.

NOW, TO HELP ROUND OUT THIS PICTURE LET'S GET SOME MORE UNDERSTANDING OF HOW THE LORD GOD MADE ADAM IN THE GARDEN OF EDEN.

> **And the LORD God formed man [of] the dust of the ground, and breathed into his nostrils the breath of life; and man became a living soul.**
> **Genesis 2:7 KJV**

So the LORD God made a physical body from the dust or more literally the clay of the earth, but it was a lifeless body. Then, He breathed the breath of life into the nostrils and the man was no longer a lifeless body, but became a living soul. It is important to note that the breath of life in man is the spirit of man that is given by the Spirit of God.

The Spirit of God hath made me, and the breath of the Almighty hath given me life.
Job 33:4 KJV

Now a body on its own is not a living soul, and neither is the spirit of man without a body a living soul. It's a bit like a math equation… A body plus a spirit equals a living soul.

body + spirit = living soul

Now let's think about this. If a body plus a spirit equals a living soul, what is going to happen if you break or crush either the body or the spirit? You guessed it, it will no longer equal a living soul. There may be an existent soul, but not a living soul the way God intended from the beginning.

body + ~~spirit~~ = ~~living soul~~

I understand there are varying levels of a broken heart and the severity of how it affects a person's

Identifying A Broken Heart

life has varying degrees. It is obvious that a person is still in the land of the living while they have a broken heart, otherwise, there would be no opportunity to heal from a broken heart and find life again, so don't go black and white with this example. I simply want to show you how important our heart is to our life both on the inside and outside. Ultimately it will be a great hindrance to the life of God in us by His Spirit to issue forth if our heart is broken. Our Father knows this.

He knows that when He calls an individual to Himself through the preaching of the good news of Yeshua our Messiah there is often a heart that first needs healing from the cruelty of sin in the world that brings reproaches, hurts, and losses. He knows that for us to experience and share His life by the Holy Spirit, and to be an effective and functioning part of establishing the Kingdom of God on earth in the future we need our hearts healed. This is why when Yeshua began His ministry here on earth, He began by getting up in a weekly Shabbat service at the synagogue He attended and read from the scroll of Isaiah and this is what He read:

The Spirit of the Lord [is] upon me, because he hath anointed me to preach the gospel to the poor; he hath sent me to heal the brokenhearted, to preach deliverance to the captives, and recovering of sight to the blind, to set at liberty them that are bruised, To preach the acceptable year of the Lord.
Luke 4:18-19 KJV

If we go back to Isaiah 61, from which Yeshua was reading, we will see why the Father anointed Him and sent Him to do these works in the lives of people.

The Spirit of the Lord GOD [is] upon me; because the LORD hath anointed me to preach good tidings unto the meek; he hath sent me to bind up the brokenhearted, to proclaim liberty to the captives, and the opening of the prison to

Identifying A Broken Heart

[them that are] bound; To proclaim the acceptable year of the LORD, and the day of vengeance of our God; to comfort all that mourn; To appoint unto them that mourn in Zion, to give unto them beauty for ashes, the oil of joy for mourning, the garment of praise for the spirit of heaviness; <u>that they might be called trees of righteousness, the planting of the LORD, that he might be glorified. And they shall build the old wastes, they shall raise up the former desolations, and they shall repair the waste cities, the desolations of many generations.</u>
Isaiah 61:1-4 KJV (underlined added)

From what Yeshua read in context, we can begin to understand that the ultimate purpose for healing the brokenhearted, among other works, is to prepare a people to rebuild and restore this planet in righteousness from the devastation of sin in the Messianic Kingdom to come.

This insight will take us into the next chapter, but before we go there I simply want to mention one more thing. I am a person just like you. Everything I teach is something that our Father has taught me from the Scriptures by His Spirit to help guide me in the journey of my own heart being healed. I have been called many things in the Body of Messiah and held varying positions. I have been called: pastor, teacher, deacon, board member, and most recently a Messianic rabbi. However, at the end of the day, I am just a son of God by faith in Yeshua learning to be more like Yeshua.

I really believe the reason I have held these positions in the Body of Messiah and am even writing this book is because I have one simple perspective and that is this: If I am going to set out on the journey to learn about the ways of God, His blessings, and His healing for mankind I might as well take others along with me. That is truly all I am doing.

Identifying A Broken Heart

Take your time reading this book. I have aimed to make it simple and clear, but at times the truths will hit hard and deep. Be honest with yourself and be honest with God. The healing of the broken heart is not neat and clean cut. It's messy and truly only for those who are totally committed to being healed not just for themselves in order to have a better day, but to serve Him and to be able to bring life to others in a world that desperately needs their hearts healed too.

Chapter 2

Healing the Broken Heart: A Messianic Mandate

If you are reading this book, then you are probably interested in helping the brokenhearted heal, or you may be struggling with a broken heart. Perhaps it's both.

In Luke 4:16-21 we read that when Yeshua was ready to reveal His identity to those in His hometown of Nazareth, He went into the synagogue He had grown up going to on Shabbat, and as was His custom, stood up to read out of the scroll of the prophet Isaiah. He opened the scroll to the section we know today as Isaiah 61:1-2a and began to read:

"The Spirit of the LORD [is] upon Me, Because He has anointed Me To preach the gospel to [the] poor; He has sent Me to heal the brokenhearted, To proclaim liberty to [the] captives And recovery of sight to [the] blind, To set at liberty those who are oppressed; To proclaim the acceptable year of the LORD."
Luke 4:18-19 NKJV

Then Yeshua goes on to say:

And He began to say to them, "Today this Scripture is fulfilled in your hearing." Luke 4:21 NKJV

Why did Yeshua do this? Why did He read these particular Scriptures to those attending the synagogue in His hometown? It's quite simple... He was publicly stating from the prophets His mandate from the Father as the Anointed (Meshiach) One of Israel. Yeshua was going to do things mankind had never seen before in miracles, signs, wonders, deliverance, healing the brokenhearted, and giving mankind a demonstration and taste of the Kingdom of God to come on earth. He was going to preach the good news of the Kingdom, the forgiveness of sins. He was going to preach and teach judgment and His return as King of the whole earth.

If you are at all familiar with the books of Matthew, Mark, Luke, and John then you know this is exactly what Yeshua did during His earthly ministry. In fact, if we go to the very last verse in the book of John, it states:

And there are also many other things that Jesus did, which if they were written one by one, I suppose that even the world itself could not contain the books that would be written. Amen. John 21:25 NKJV

When John the Baptist sent some of his disciples to go and question Yeshua as to whether or not He was the one that should come or should they look for another, listen to how Yeshua answered him.

And when John had heard in prison about the works of Christ, he sent two of his disciples and said to Him, "Are You the Coming One, or do we look for another?" Jesus answered and said to them, "Go and tell John the things which you

> **hear and see: "[The] blind see and [the] lame walk; [the] lepers are cleansed and [the] deaf hear; [the] dead are raised up and [the] poor have the gospel preached to them.**
> **Matthew 11:2-5 NKJV**

What Yeshua was implying by His answer to John's disciples is that you will know whether or not I am the One by the things I do, because the things I do were the things spoken of me to do by the prophets. It was the mandate of the Messiah (the anointed one), according to the will of the Father, to be done in the power of the Holy Spirit.

> **how God anointed Jesus of Nazareth with the Holy Spirit and with power, who went about doing good and healing all who were oppressed by the devil, for God was with Him.**
> **Acts 10:38 NKJV**

I think at this point it is clear that Yeshua had a mandate to do all that was said of the Messiah in Isaiah 61:1-2,

> **"The Spirit of the Lord GOD [is] upon Me, Because the LORD has anointed Me To preach good tidings to the poor; He has sent Me to heal the brokenhearted, To proclaim liberty to the captives, And the opening of the prison to [those who are] bound; To proclaim the acceptable year of the LORD, And the day of vengeance of our God; To comfort all who mourn,**
> **Isaiah 61:1-2 NKJV**

BUT WHAT ABOUT THE BODY OF MESSIAH? DO WE HAVE THE SAME MANDATE?

To answer that, let's look to the Scriptures, as always. In John 14:12, Yeshua says something to His disciples that is quite interesting, quite challenging, and often misinterpreted.

Most assuredly, I say to you, he who believes in Me, the works that I do he will do also; and greater [works] than these he will do, because I go to My Father.
John 14:12 NKJV

Let's slow down and look at what Yeshua said a little more closely. He says, "He that believeth on me..." Stop there. What does it mean if someone believes in Yeshua? Among other things beyond the scope of this teaching, it means they are a member of the Body of Messiah through faith in His atonement for our sins and His resurrection from the dead. The next phrase indicates what a member of the Body of Messiah will be able to do and should do. That phrase is, "The works that I do shall he do also." What are those works? They are the works Yeshua was mandated to do in Isaiah 61:1-2.

To make it a little easier to remember, let's write each one of those works out in a list. I have taken the liberty to reword them a bit for the sake of interpretation:

THE BODY OF MESSIAH IS ABLE TO AND SHOULD DO

1. **Preach the good news of the Kingdom**
2. **Heal the broken-hearted**
3. **Preach liberty to those in bondage**
4. **Then be able to open the prison door to those in bondage**
5. **Preach that Yeshua will come again to establish the Kingdom of Israel**
6. **Preach that He will also judge the quick and dead. Vengeance will come to those not found worthy to inherit the Kingdom**

These are the works Yeshua did, and so we should also do the same works. Then He goes on to say, "And greater works than these shall he do because I go unto my Father". Wait, what does that mean? Does it mean we will do more amazing miracles than Yeshua? Well, some do interpret it that way, but to me, it makes much more sense to interpret this as saying that the amount of work done will be more numerous, and the language makes room for that. Think about it; Yeshua says He is going back to His Father, so He will not be around to do the works anymore. Besides, think of some of the miracles Yeshua did... Fed thousands of people with a couple of loaves of bread and fish, walked on water, and instantly calmed the storm at sea. Personally, I am not against people having faith in doing these things, but I have also not heard of anyone else doing these things before. However, I have, in the power of the Holy Spirit, seen people healed of diseases, delivered from evil spirits, and miracles done in human bodies. Ultimately, Yeshua did not come to earth to calm seas or walk on water but to destroy the works of the devil.

> **He who sins is of the devil, for the devil has sinned from the beginning. For this purpose the Son of God was manifested, that He might destroy the works of the devil.**
> **1 John 3:8 NKJV**

So the works we are to do that He did represent destroying the works of the devil in the lives of other people. This would include broken hearts, torment from evil spirits, and physical healing.

> **how God anointed Jesus of Nazareth with the Holy Spirit and with power, who went about doing good and healing all who were oppressed by the devil, for God was with Him.**
> **Acts 10:38 NKJV**

So my understanding is that because we are not going back to the Father yet, we as the Body of Messiah will continue to be around and do more of these works that Yeshua did. He was isolated due to His geographical location and 3½ years of ministry.

Members of the Body of Messiah are all over the world and usually have much longer than 3½ years to minister. What I believe is being conveyed is that members of the Body of Messiah will do the same works and more of them.

WHY IS IT SIGNIFICANT THAT YESHUA WENT UNTO THE FATHER? AND WHAT DID HE GIVE US WHEN HE WENT?

Lastly, in this verse, I want to talk about the phrase, "Because I go unto my Father". Why is this statement really significant in our discussion? In John 16:7, Yeshua said this:

> **Nevertheless I tell you the truth; It is expedient for you that I go away: for if I go not away, the Comforter will not come unto you; but if I depart, I will send him unto you.**
> **John 16:7 KJV**

Earlier in John 7:38-39, on the last day of Sukkot (The Feast of Tabernacles), Yeshua proclaimed what will happen in the future for those that believe in Him:

> **On the last day, that great [day] of the feast, Jesus stood and cried out, saying, "If anyone thirsts, let him come to Me and drink. "He who believes in Me, as the Scripture has said, out of his heart will flow rivers of living water." But this He spoke concerning the Spirit, whom those believing in Him would receive; for the Holy Spirit was not yet [given], because Jesus was not yet glorified.**
> **John 7:37-39 NKJV**

Do you see why it was important for Yeshua to go to His Father? Because the Holy Spirit would not fill believers until He had ascended to be with His Father. That same Holy Spirit that anointed Yeshua to fulfill the mandate of Isaiah 61:1-2.

So what happened when the time finally came for Yeshua to ascend to His Father? In Acts 1, Yeshua instructed His disciples to stay in Jerusalem to wait for the promise of the Father, which was and is the Holy Spirit.

> **And being assembled together with [them], He commanded them not to depart from Jerusalem, but to wait for the Promise of the Father, "which," [He said], "you have heard from Me; for John truly baptized with water, but you shall be baptized with the Holy Spirit not many days from now."**
> **Acts 1:4-5 NKJV**

Then the last thing He tells them before He is taken up to be with His Father is:

> **And He said to them, "It is not for you to know times or seasons which the Father has put in His own authority.** (Yeshua said this because they asked if the kingdom of Israel would be restored.)

But you shall receive power when the Holy Spirit has come upon you; and you shall be witnesses to Me in Jerusalem, and in all Judea and Samaria, and to the end of the earth."
Acts 1:7-8 NKJV (parenthesis mine)

So Yeshua tells them that there are certain things, such as His return to establish the Kingdom in Israel, that they will have no power over, but only God the Father. However, when they are immersed in the Holy Spirit, they will receive power to become witnesses of Yeshua in Israel and all over the world.

WHAT DOES IT MEAN TO BE A WITNESS?

A correct understanding of this is very important to answering the question of whether or not the mandate Yeshua was given is now our mandate in the Body of Messiah. A witness, by definition, is an individual who can attest to and/or prove that specific reported events did indeed occur or that specific individuals were present and involved in the events. But people like you and me have never seen Yeshua, so is this verse for us? It has to be because the disciples He was talking to never made it to the uttermost ends of the earth... We, as the Body of Messiah, have. In Acts 1:7-8, it is clear that there is a connection between the power of the Holy Spirit and the ability to be an effective witness for Yeshua.

Today, in the Body of Messiah, when people talk about witnessing, it is usually in the context of telling people ABOUT Yeshua, not DOING what Yeshua did. Do not get me wrong, it is wonderful to tell someone about Yeshua, but does that really prove to someone that Yeshua was and is who He said He was and is?

Think about it... What if you were telling someone about Yeshua and how He healed people? Well, that person might think it sounds great, but then ask the question, "How do you know that isn't just a made-up story?" What if you could respond back by saying, "Yeshua healed that person by the power of the Holy Spirit, and the same Holy Spirit that was in Him to do the works has been given to me to do the same thing." Then, you, by the power of the Holy Spirit, healed someone.

You would have just become a real-time, present witness of Yeshua and His claims by being able to do the same things He did. This does not make us the Messiah or "little gods"; none of us have ever or ever will die for the sins of the world, but it does make us a witness to Yeshua as we are instructed to be because we are able to do the same works He did.

SO DOES THE BODY OF MESSIAH HAVE A MANDATE TO DO THE WORKS OF ISAIAH 61:1-2?

Absolutely, it is clear that the mandate our Lord and Savior was given by the Father, has now been given to His Body to continue according to the will of the Father in the power of the Holy Spirit.

> **And as you go, preach, saying, 'The kingdom of heaven is at hand.' "Heal the sick, cleanse the lepers, raise the dead, cast out demons. Freely you have received, freely give.**
> **Matthew 10:7-8 NKJV**

Now, let's review our list of what that mandate is.

THE BODY OF MESSIAH CAN AND SHOULD DO.

1. **Preach the good news of the Kingdom**
2. **Heal the broken-hearted**
3. **Preach liberty to those in bondage**
4. **Then be able to open the prison door to those in bondage**
5. **Preach that Yeshua will come again to establish the Kingdom to Israel**

6. **Preach that He will also judge the quick and dead. Vengeance will come to those not found worthy to inherit the Kingdom**

Which of these do you see operating in the Body of Messiah today? I am going to be honest: I have been around the Body of Messiah for 20 years. I have been in Reformed, Methodist, Charismatic, Prophetic, Baptist, and Messianic circles during that time. I have helped and ministered to people who were Mennonite, Amish, Catholic, you name it! I see that the Body of Messiah overall does preach the good news! I also observe there is a constant message of Yeshua returning and the doctrine of judgment to come, although this doctrine is being spoken of less and less. And yes, most people in the Body of Messiah are very compassionate and do offer comfort to those who are hurting. All of this is wonderful, but it does not complete the mandate.

It has been my observation in 20 years of ministry that there is a lack of understanding in the Body of

Messiah at large in how to heal the broken heart, which is the basis for the next two works, which are preaching liberty to captives and opening the door to those in prison.

IT TAKES MORE THAN PRAYER

I do not mean to sound harsh, but a simple prayer is not going to get the job done when it comes to healing a broken heart. It takes a working knowledge of the Scriptures and an understanding of truth that will help ministers discern how to address the issues and spiritual dynamics in play in a person's life and the power of the Holy Spirit to deal with those issues.

Again, a broken heart is not simply an emotional issue that causes various problems relationally and psychologically, but is the result of something people do not always think about from day to day, and that is the war for the heart of man between God and satan!

This book is for those who are helping and ministering to the broken-hearted, but also for those who are feeling lost, discouraged, heavy, and simply not understanding why a breakthrough seems to elude them. This book is certainly not an exhaustive insight into all the issues surrounding the broken heart, but I do believe that the insights contained in this book are able to set an individual on the right path to having their heart healed or help those who are ministering to the brokenhearted.

Chapter 3

One War, Two Kingdoms

TWO TYPES OF PEOPLE

If you live in the Northeastern region of the United States, you may have heard of a grocery store named Wegmans. There are grocery stores, and then there is Wegmans! If you know, you know, but I digress. We lived just outside of Rochester, NY, for a couple of years, which happens to be where Wegmans is headquartered, and they had a location around the corner from us that we would frequent pretty often.

My wife Kassy and I have five amazing children, and I have always sought to instill character within them. One of the ways I have gone about doing this is by making a big deal regarding taking responsibility for what many in society deem small things. For example, a firm handshake, looking someone in the eye, opening doors for the elderly, being a good neighbor, and perhaps the biggest one in my book, putting your shopping cart in the designated return area! I will admit, and my friends and family will attest, that I am a little overboard on this one.

One day, we took a family trip to Wegmans. Once finished, we were loading into our van when I looked out the front windshield and saw that a shopping cart had been haphazardly stranded in the parking space in front of me rather than properly returned to the designated return area.

I was in a fun-loving mood, and jokingly (but kinda serious) stated in a loud voice for all the car to hear, "Kids there are two types of people in the world: Those that put their shopping carts in the designated return areas and those that leave them around the parking lot not considering how that may affect others". I said, "At any moment an unsuspecting driver of a car who just wants to park and enjoy their Wegmans experience might pull in here having not seen the shopping cart and hit it and dent their car." So I did what any person with a moral compass would do: I got out and returned a shopping cart that I didn't use for someone else. But the best part of this sequence of events was that just as I pushed the shopping cart out of the parking space, a car came whipping into that spot and would have surely collided with this stranded shopping cart. I looked back at my children, giving them a face that said "You see?" and thinking to myself that this could not have gone better. When I returned to the van, my children were in disbelief and were convinced I somehow planned the whole thing. It was a great memory, and since then, I have been even more vocal about returning your shopping cart after you are done using it.

It's a fun story, and yes, taking responsibility for the little things does matter in life, but I don't actually think we can truly place everyone in the world into one of two categories based on whether or not they consistently return their shopping cart. Perhaps there are little things you feel strongly about or pet peeves where you might be tempted to place everyone in one of two categories, but life is more complicated than that. Maybe someone could not return a shopping cart because of health reasons, or maybe they received an emergency call as they were walking out of the store; we don't always know. The reality is that some people who consistently return their shopping carts will not inherit eternal life, so what does that badge even accomplish for you?

The only two categories in which every single human being that has ever lived fits into one or the other are these:

1. **Those who are the citizens of the Kingdom of God and obedient to its ruler, Yeshua.**
2. **Those who are citizens of the kingdom of darkness and obedient to its ruler, satan.**

ONE WAR, BETWEEN TWO KINGDOMS

Amid all the wars we see, be it nation against nation or individual against individual, there is really only one war between two kingdoms. And everyone you know is a member of one kingdom or the other.

Everything we see wrong in the world today, whether it be abortion, gender confusion, wars, divorce, division in the Body of Messiah, fatherlessness, the drug epidemic, backbiting politics, or even fallen pastors, is happening because there is a war over one thing between two opposing kingdoms. And you and I are in it whether we realize it or not. Our lives and our generations hang in the balance.

> **For we do not wrestle against flesh and blood, but against principalities, against powers, against the rulers of the darkness of this age, against spiritual [hosts] of wickedness in the heavenly [places].**
> **Ephesians 6:12 NKJV**

To be clear, this chapter will not exhaustively cover all the Bible teaches regarding spiritual warfare;

however, my main objective for this chapter is to demystify spiritual warfare. So many believers today are yelling at the devil, stomping their feet, and declaring their victory, but really, in doing all of that, they are just throwing spiritual punches hoping to land a blow to an invisible enemy. Spiritual warfare is not a guessing game, it is won according to knowledge applied with faith. Look at what Paul said:

> **Therefore I run thus: not with uncertainty. Thus I fight: not as [one who] beats the air.**
> **1 Corinthians 9:26 NKJV**

We need to understand who and what we are fighting and do so according to our knowledge. So I want to paint a picture for you from the Scriptures of what you and I cannot see with our physical eyes but are dealing with everyday. When we can begin to understand our journey in the context of this war between two kingdoms, we are able to take responsibility and resist deceptions, lies, and wiles the enemy designs to cause trouble and destruction in our lives, including the broken heart.

Let me ask you a question. If you are a believer in Yeshua, having repented of sin and trusting in Him for the forgiveness of sins and the resurrection from the dead, what was the first thing that happened when you first believed? You may not have realized it at the time, I certainly didn't, but the first thing that happens when a person becomes a believer is found in Colossians 1:12-14.

Giving thanks unto the Father, which hath made us meet to be partakers of the inheritance of the saints in light: Who hath delivered us from the power of darkness, and hath translated [us] into the kingdom of his dear Son: In whom we have redemption through his blood, [even] the forgiveness of sins:
Colossians 1:12-14 KJV

Do you see what happened? You changed which kingdom you were a member of. You changed kingdoms. One day, you were a member of satan's kingdom, knowingly or ignorantly, but the day you put your trust in Yeshua, you became a citizen of the Kingdom of God rather than the kingdom of darkness. Amazing, isn't it?

Each one of these kingdoms produces fruit based on the desire of its ruler for its citizens and the character of its ruler. Yeshua is the ruler of the Kingdom of God, and satan is the ruler of the kingdom of darkness. Let's see which fruit each produces in their citizens.

> **"The thief does not come except to steal, and to kill, and to destroy. I have come that they may have life, and that they may have [it] more abundantly.**
> **John 10:10 NKJV**

We are even able to observe how this works in modern nations today. When a nation is led by a despot or dictator, the average citizen struggles with poverty, hunger, and constant fear of doing something that would offend the leader in such a way that could cost them their or a family member's life. Oftentimes, despots will outlaw religion of any kind, leaving their citizens without faith, hope, and purpose. North Korea and the Kim family would be prime modern-day examples of this reality.

Conversely, even though there is no such thing as perfect human government, when the aim of the leader(s) of a nation is to defend and preserve liberties and intrinsic human rights for their citizens, the people will flourish as a whole. If earthly rulers can have this type of impact on their citizens for good or evil, just imagine what type of impact the rulers of these two kingdoms we are discussing have on their citizens.

One War, Two Kingdoms

WHERE DOES SPIRITUAL WARFARE BEGIN?

I have heard it numerous times over the years, and I have probably said it myself, that spiritual warfare begins on your knees, in prayer. Well, we certainly fight many spiritual battles in prayer, but is that where spiritual warfare really begins? Let's take a look at Mark 1:21-27 and see if there is something more than just prayer when it comes to exercising authority over satan and his kingdom.

> **Then they went into Capernaum, and immediately on the Sabbath He entered the synagogue and taught. And they were astonished at His teaching, for He taught them as one having authority, and not as the scribes. Now there was a man in their synagogue with an unclean spirit. And he cried out, saying, "Let [us] alone! What have we to do with You, Jesus of Nazareth? Did You come to destroy us? I know who You are--the Holy One of God!" But Jesus rebuked him, saying, "Be quiet, and come**

> out of him!" And when the unclean spirit had convulsed him and cried out with a loud voice, he came out of him. Then they were all amazed, so that they questioned among themselves, saying, "What is this? What new doctrine [is] this? For with authority He commands even the unclean spirits, and they obey Him."
> Mark 1:21-27 NKJV

To bring some context to the passage, this is the first record of Yeshua casting out an evil spirit during His earthly ministry. Quite interesting where He did it too... In a synagogue! But that is a side note. Did you happen to catch what the people called this event? Let's look again at the last verse.

> Then they were all amazed, so that they questioned among themselves, saying, "What is this? What new doctrine [is] this? For with authority He commands even the unclean spirits, and they obey Him."
> Mark 1:27 NKJV

They called this spiritual warfare in which Yeshua exercised authority over satan's kingdom a doctrine!

The doctrine being spoken of by these attendees of the weekly Shabbat service was the doctrine of setting the prisoners free, found in Isaiah 61.

> **The Spirit of the Lord GOD [is] upon Me, Because the LORD has anointed Me To preach good tidings to the poor; He has sent Me to heal the brokenhearted, To proclaim liberty to the captives, And the opening of the prison to [those who are] bound;**
> **Isaiah 61:1 NKJV**

By Yeshua demonstrating this doctrine by the power of the Holy Spirit, He was giving a greater understanding that by the power of the Holy Spirit, an evil spirit could be commanded to leave an individual that was bound by it.

And this doctrine was not just for the first century. I have also followed this doctrine by faith and seen evil spirits leave people, and in turn, they were freed from bondage. Sometimes there have been physical manifestations like it says in Mark 1, and other times there may have just been some tears or even nothing at all. I don't always know what happens at the moment, but it has been amazing over the years to have people approach me 6 weeks, 6 months, a year, or two years after I commanded an evil spirit to leave them and hear their testimony of being set free. Some were in bondage to night terrors, others had physical ailments, and some had been healed of psychological diagnoses such as OCD, Depression, and PTSD because of the ministry. But remember, it is a doctrine, not prayer.

Luke 11:20 says,

"But if I cast out demons with the finger of God, surely the kingdom of God has come upon you.
Luke 11:20 NKJV

We know at this point that casting out evil spirits is a doctrine, but is that all there is to this doctrine? According to the verse above, what does it mean if an evil spirit is cast out by the finger of God (the Holy Spirit)? It means that the Kingdom of God has come upon an individual, meaning that the Kingdom of God was more powerful than the kingdom of satan and proved it by driving it out.

So, spiritual warfare does not begin in prayer but in doctrine. And what is the doctrine in concise terms? Based on Isaiah 61:1 and other accompanying Scriptures from the Tenakh (Old Testament), when the Messiah came, (Yeshua is the Messiah) He by the power of the Holy Spirit, could overpower the kingdom of satan with the Kingdom of God. When this happens, the bad fruit of satan's kingdom, like oppression, depression, fear, works of the flesh, physical infirmities, and the like, fades away. Then the good fruit of the Kingdom of God begins to blossom. The fruit that blossoms is the fruit found in Galatians 5:22 among other Scriptures.

> **But the fruit of the Spirit is love, joy, peace, longsuffering, kindness, goodness, faithfulness, gentleness, self-control. Against such there is no law.**
> **Galatians 5:22-23 NKJV**

WHAT IS AT STAKE IN THIS WAR?

Every war in history is fought over something or someone. Oftentimes, wars are fought over land, government structure, or religious establishment in any given area. But what is at stake in this war, between the Kingdom of God and the kingdom of satan, is **the human heart.** Why? Because it is with the heart we obey one kingdom or another.

Let's look at Romans 6:15-19

> What then? Shall we sin because we are not under law but under grace? Certainly not! Do you not know that to whom you present yourselves slaves to obey, you are that one's slaves whom you obey, whether of sin [leading] to death, or of obedience [leading] to righteousness? But God be thanked that [though] you were slaves of sin, yet you obeyed from the heart that form of doctrine to which you were delivered. And having been set free from sin, you became slaves of righteousness. I speak in human [terms] because of the weakness of your flesh. For just as you presented your members [as] slaves of uncleanness, and of lawlessness [leading] to [more] lawlessness, so now present your members [as] slaves [of] righteousness for holiness.
> **Romans 6:15-19 NKJV**

Before we get into this passage, I want to highlight the disclaimer Paul gives when he says, "I speak in human terms because of the weakness of your flesh". The human term he is using is the word "slave". He is not trying to say we are slaves to God, particularly in the way we think of slaves. Slaves are nothing more than property, with little to no rights. We absolutely serve God, but we are not His slaves; rather, we are sons and daughters of God if we believe in Yeshua, His Son, as our Lord and Savior.

But as many as received Him, to them He gave the right to become children of God, to those who believe in His name:
John 1:12 NKJV

However, he is using the terminology of a slave because this would have been a context his listeners and readers would have understood in their day. In this war between two kingdoms, there are two masters, and whichever one we obey, not confess, but obey is our master.

Now, if we continue through this passage, we come to verses 17-18, which states:

But God be thanked that [though] you were slaves of sin, yet you obeyed from the heart that form of doctrine to which you were delivered. And having been set free from sin, you became slaves of righteousness.
Romans 6:17-18 NKJV

According to this verse, how is it that we are able to be delivered from the grip of satan's kingdom into the liberty of the Kingdom of God? **Obeying from the heart.** In context, how could we be under the bondage of satan's kingdom and not live in the freedom of God's Kingdom? By obeying satan and his kingdom in the heart, even ignorantly.

DO YOU NOW SEE WHY OUR HEART IS IN THE MIDDLE OF THIS WAR BETWEEN TWO KINGDOMS?

This is why there are so many Scriptures that exhort us to have truth upon, in, and written on our hearts. What is in our heart determines how we will speak and how we will act. Will it be speech and action that gives witness to the Kingdom of God to come on earth ruled by Yeshua, or does it give witness to satan's counterfeit kingdom that wants to overthrow the true Kingdom?

When Yeshua comes back to rule and reign from Mt. Zion in Jerusalem (Micah 4:7, Psalm 2:6) there is a specific type of person that will be able to dwell with Him there when He establishes the Kingdom of God on earth and all the kingdoms in the world will come under His rulership and the Kingdom of God (Revelation. 11:15).

LORD, who may abide in Your tabernacle? Who may dwell in Your holy hill? He who walks uprightly, And works righteousness, And speaks the truth in his heart;
Psalm 15:1-2 NKJV

Walking uprightly and working righteousness, which represents our actions that show whom we obey, is tied directly to speaking truth in one's heart.

WHAT IS OBEDIENCE TO THE TRUTH?

What do I mean when I say obedience to the truth? Well, what is truth? Forgive the briefness of such a deep subject, but in a nutshell, the truth is what God has said, in particular, what He has said He would do. He told Abram, later known as Abraham, that He would cause the promised seed to come forth from Abram's loins, and later God promised more specifically this seed would come forth from his wife Sarah's womb. What was obedience in this situation for Abram?

> **And he believed in the LORD, and He accounted it to him for righteousness.**
> **Genesis 15:6 NKJV**

When Abram believed what God promised, it was counted as righteousness to him, and Abram was obedient. Many people make the mistake of thinking the gospel frees us from obedience. Actually, the only way the gospel has any positive impact on our lives is to obey the gospel and establish obedience to the faith of the gospel.

> **For the time [has come] for judgment to begin at the house of God; and if [it begins] with us first, what will [be] the end of those who do not obey the gospel of God?**
> **1 Peter 4:17 NKJV**

> **Through Him we have received grace and apostleship for obedience to the faith among all**

**nations for His name, among whom you also are the called of Jesus Christ;
Romans 1:5-6 NKJV**

Obedience to the truth is believing and trusting the promises and covenants of God to mankind for our good. The preeminent obedience is our belief and trust that God the Father sent His Son to die and atone for our sins so that we may be forgiven of our sins. Also, believing and trusting that Yeshua, because He lived a sinless life, death has no right to Him and the Holy Spirit raised Him from the dead and will also raise us from the dead in the first resurrection.

Moreover, brethren, I declare to you the gospel which I preached to you, which also you received and in which you stand, by which also you are saved, if you hold fast that word which I preached to you--unless you believed in vain. For I delivered to you first of all that which I also

received: that Christ died for our sins according to the Scriptures,
1 Corinthians 15:1-3 NKJV

We must understand that believing this with our heart IS obedience to the truth because it is what God promised long ago through the prophets and came to pass in the life of Yeshua. And it is when we believe this with the heart that we change kingdoms.

giving thanks to the Father who has qualified us to be partakers of the inheritance of the saints in the light. He has delivered us from the power of darkness and conveyed [us] into the kingdom of the Son of His love, in whom we have redemption through His blood, the forgiveness of sins.
Colossians 1:12-14 NKJV

RESTORING REPENTANCE TO THE KINGDOM OF GOD

I am not sure about you, but when I first became a believer, I had no idea what repentance meant. People were telling me to repent, but no one really took the time to explain to me what I would be doing by repenting. I struggled with this term, even though I was learning about what it meant in Greek and Hebrew, but I still did not understand exactly what I was doing when I repented other than trying not to sin and, in turn, be a doer of the Word.

The Greek word most often translated as repent is "metanoeo". It literally means a change of mind and heart. We don't find the word repent too many times in the Tenakh (Old Testament), only 8 times in most English translations, but we do find the word "turn". In Hebrew, this is the word "t'shuv". This is the word used when the LORD, through the prophets, would call Israel to turn (t'shuv) from idols and turn back (t'shuv) to Him, the Living God.

From these definitions, we can understand that repentance is changing our minds and hearts regarding our lives, turning away from sin and turning toward God.

But what is really happening when we repent? Well, let's go back and look at the original message of John the Baptist, Yeshua, and the apostles. What was their primary message?

In those days John the Baptist came preaching in the wilderness of Judea, and saying, "Repent, for the kingdom of heaven is at hand!"
Matthew 3:1-2 NKJV

From that time Jesus began to preach and to say, "Repent, for the kingdom of heaven is at hand."
Matthew 4:17 NKJV

These twelve Jesus sent out and commanded them, saying: "Do not go into the way of the Gentiles, and do not enter a city of the Samaritans. "But go rather to the lost sheep of

the house of Israel. "And as you go, preach, saying, 'The kingdom of heaven is at hand.' Matthew 10:5-7 NKJV

The primary message was to repent, for the Kingdom of God is at hand. What does that mean? It means that those hearing the message have been under the bondage of satan's kingdom knowingly or unknowingly, and to turn from obeying satan and conducting their lives according to his kingdom and rather turn to God the Father and His Son, Yeshua, and live your life according to the ways of His Kingdom. The message was to change kingdoms and change your citizenship. Why? Because satan's kingdom will be destroyed, and that includes all who obey it. God did not and does not today want any to perish in that destruction, but we must change kingdoms by repenting and turning to the Kingdom of God.

The Lord is not slack concerning [His] promise, as some count slackness, but is longsuffering

toward us, not willing that any should perish but that all should come to repentance.

2 Peter 3:9 NKJV

A great example of repentance is one that is very personal in my family tree. My great-grandfather, Abraham Levitsky, was a Yiddish-speaking Jewish man who owned and ran a beet sugar refinery with his family in Kyiv, Ukraine, in the late 1800s. In those days, Czar Nicholas ll would persecute the Jews of Russia and Ukraine and had the power to conscript Jewish men into his army. My great-grandfather was one of them. During a conflict in Turkey, my great-grandfather was taken prisoner as a POW. The details are unknown, but this turned out to be a blessing because he was able to escape prison, service in the Czar's army, and immigrate to the United States in 1907 a couple of years behind his wife who immigrated in 1905 while pregnant with my grandfather.

One War, Two Kingdoms

What's interesting is that I have access to some of the paperwork Abraham had to fill out upon coming to the United States, and what really struck me was what he had to renounce and then pledge his loyalty to. In the document, it reads

It is my bona fide intention to renounce forever all allegiance and fidelity to any foreign prince, potentate, state, or sovereignty, and particularly to the present government of Russia, of whom I am now a subject; I arrived at the port of New York in the state of New York on the 24th day of May, anno Domini 1907; I am not an anarchist; I am not a polygamist nor a believer in the practice of polygamy; and it is my intention in good faith to become a citizen of the United States of America and to permanently reside therein: SO HELP ME GOD. (Signature to follow)

This perfectly demonstrates repentance from satan's kingdom to the Kingdom of God. We must renounce all allegiance to that kingdom and its government, which is satan. We must renounce all ways of conduct in the kingdom that are not allowed in God's kingdom. We make a firm commitment and decision to serve God, His Kingdom, and learn how to walk in the ways of the Kingdom.

Please give yourself time to learn to be a proper citizen of the Kingdom of God. In fact, it is a lifetime journey, so don't allow the enemy to beat you up if you recognize areas you still operate as if you were in satan's kingdom in some areas of life. When a person moves to a new country and gets their citizenship, they are 100% a citizen, but it doesn't mean they totally know how to conduct themselves as a citizen of that country. There are different laws, customs, and cultures, and that takes time. Learning how to be a citizen of the Kingdom of God is called sanctification, and it is done little by little with the occasional big leap.

RESTORING A KINGDOM MESSAGE

I really believe the Body of Messiah needs the Kingdom message restored. We have a forgiveness message and an eternal life message, but to what end? Just to go to a mystical heaven? There is a Kingdom in Heaven, and one day that Kingdom is coming to earth, we will be raised from the dead and will be a part of the functioning Kingdom under Yeshua the King. This is why we repent, this is why we obey the truth, and the war satan wages is an attempt to prevent that from happening and us inheriting it.

So many today are crying out for healing and deliverance, but healing is not just healing, and deliverance is not just deliverance. When someone is healed and delivered, what actually happened is one Kingdom came and overthrew another kingdom in a person's heart and life. **And this is how the broken heart is healed...** As we will see later in this book, satan's kingdom breaks hearts, but the Kingdom of God heals hearts.

HOW DO YOU SEE YOUR LIFE NOW?

Most of you were probably not expecting a chapter in a book about healing the broken heart to radically challenge your worldview, but it is vital to the healing of the broken heart. Most of us who have had our hearts broken probably chalked it up to someone doing us wrong, our inability to handle emotions, just getting a bad lot, or something else in the natural sense. In reality, we are in a war, and our hearts are on the line. One kingdom wants to break our hearts so that its ruler satan can control us, and the other Kingdom wants our hearts healed so that we can obey its ruler Yeshua, who is our Maker and Creator and knows what He had in mind for us from the beginning.

From here on out, we will be uncovering how satan's kingdom attempts to break our hearts so that we will not trust God and not experience the wholeness that the Father sent Yeshua to win for us through His death and resurrection.

Healing the broken heart is never straightforward; it can get messy, but let's trust our Father. Be ready to repent and allow the Holy Spirit to heal our hearts from the lies we have believed. He does this often with mankind, and now it is your time!

He looketh upon men, and [if any] say, I have sinned, and perverted [that which was] right, and it profited me not; He will deliver his soul from going into the pit, and his life shall see the light. Lo, all these [things] worketh God oftentimes with man, To bring back his soul from the pit, to be enlightened with the light of the living.
Job 33:27-30 KJV

Chapter 4

The "Pain" Of A Broken Heart

The "Pain" Of A Broken Heart

THAT HURT, BUT NOT LIKE THAT KIND OF HURT...

Why is it that when an individual is dealing with a broken heart they will often explain their current state using descriptors of physical pain? Let's look at some simple examples: "When they mocked me it *hurt* so much", "Losing them has been the most *painful* experience of my life", "Them doing that to me has left me *shattered*", "When they betrayed me it was like someone *punching me in the gut*". Have you heard people say things like this before? Have you said these types of phrases before, even though there was no physical pain? Perhaps you thought these were just sayings, but there is actually a very scientific reason why people use these descriptors, and it is key to understanding the "pain" someone feels when they have a broken heart.

As we have already discussed, a broken heart is not just an emotional phenomenon. Rather, it is a wile and strategy of satan's kingdom that produces spiritual and emotional dynamics that can keep a person stuck and not experiencing life the way God designed us for us to. Remember what Proverbs 4:23 says,

Keep your heart with all diligence, For out of it [spring] the issues of life.
Proverbs 4:23 NKJV

If satan's kingdom can break our hearts, then life won't spring forth, but rather the things of death.

FORMED INTO BROKENNESS OR FORMED INTO WHOLENESS

Both life and death coming forth from the heart are not random occurrences, but we must understand this from God's original intention. Remember, we are made in the image of God.

So God created man in his [own] image, in the image of God created he him; male and female created he them.
Genesis 1:27 KJV

But because of the deception of Eve and the disobedience of Adam that caused them to eat the fruit of the knowledge of good and evil, that image was obscured by the entrance of sin into mankind. Sin corrupted how mankind now thought, spoke, and acted.

Adam and Eve were originally made perfect in the image of God. They were created to naturally think, speak, and act in a way that represented righteousness, peace, and joy with God and each other. They did not fear death because in their state before eating the fruit, they never would die. They had no strife with each other, they had no reason or temptation to lie to one another or God.

Then, after sin entered them by Adam's disobedience, they began to think, speak, and act contrary to the image they were created in.

Wherefore, as by one man sin entered into the world, and death by sin; and so death passed upon all men, for that all have sinned: Romans 5:12 KJV

In what way did they think, speak, and act differently? Well, instead of righteousness, peace, and joy, they now thought, spoke, and acted in ways that represent shame, fear, and guilt. Let's have a look back at Genesis.

So when the woman saw that the tree [was] good for food, that it [was] pleasant to the eyes, and a tree desirable to make [one] wise, she took of its fruit and ate. She also gave to her husband with her, and he ate. Then the eyes of both of them were opened, and they knew that they [were]

> **naked; and they sewed fig leaves together and made themselves coverings.**
> **Genesis 3:6-7 NKJV**

This action of making themselves coverings for their nakedness is representative of the shame they were experiencing for the first time. When we experience shame, the first response is to try to cover up the thing that we are ashamed of. People will even do this with a personality. People who present themselves over-confidently or just plain proudly are often trying to cover over something on the inside they are ashamed of and don't want others to see. We know that these coverings represented shamefulness because it says this earlier in Genesis chapter 2.

> **And they were both naked, the man and his wife, and were not ashamed.**
> **Genesis 2:25 NKJV**

So they were not ashamed of their nakedness and had no need to cover their nakedness, but then after sin entered in that changed and they covered themselves with their own devices, fig leaves.

WHAT NEXT?

And they heard the sound of the LORD God walking in the garden in the cool of the day, and Adam and his wife hid themselves from the presence of the LORD God among the trees of the garden. Then the LORD God called to Adam and said to him, "Where [are] you?" So he said, "I heard Your voice in the garden, and I was afraid because I was naked; and I hid myself." Genesis 3:8-10 NKJV

Here, we see the fear. A person only hides when they are afraid, especially when the person they are hiding from loves them and has never done anything to harm them. Adam even goes as far as to say, "I was afraid".

THEN WHAT HAPPENED?

> **And He said, "Who told you that you [were] naked? Have you eaten from the tree of which I commanded you that you should not eat?" Then the man said, "The woman whom You gave [to be] with me, she gave me of the tree, and I ate." And the LORD God said to the woman, "What [is] this you have done?" The woman said, "The serpent deceived me, and I ate."**
> **Genesis 3:11-13 NKJV**

First, let's notice that God knew something or someone had given them another image when He said, "Who told you that you were naked?" The LORD then proceeded to directly confront both Adam and Eve as to whether or not they ate the fruit, and both of them refused to take responsibility and rather blamed someone else. Adam blames Eve when he says, "It was the woman you gave me that caused me to eat," and Eve blames the serpent when she says, "The serpent deceived me and I ate". Neither one took responsibility when confronted about the issue.

Not taking responsibility and blaming others is a classic manifestation of guilt. When a person experiences guilt, they know they have done wrong, but are afraid of the consequences and therefore are too afraid to take full ownership and responsibility. Rather, they try to justify themselves by accusing others for their behavior. This interaction between them and the LORD shows the guilt they experienced.

The point is Adam and Eve were being formed into a different image than the one God created them in after His own image. Certainly, His image was still in them, but satan's kingdom was now blinding them to it through thoughts, feelings, emotions, and words and actions that would continue to defile them and others around them. This includes passing it on to the next generation.

> **But even if our gospel is veiled, it is veiled to those who are perishing, whose minds the god of this age has blinded, who do not believe, lest the light of the gospel of the glory of Christ, who is the image of God, should shine on them.**
> **2 Corinthians 4:3-4 NKJV**

A major component of the good news of Yeshua is that we can begin the process of being formed back into His image as a work of the Holy Spirit.

> **But we all, with unveiled face, beholding as in a mirror the glory of the Lord, are being transformed into the same image from glory to glory, just as by the Spirit of the Lord.**
> **2 Corinthians 3:18 NKJV**

This image being formed in man is right at the heart of the war between the two kingdoms we discussed in chapter 3. God our Father wants to form us back into His image by forming us into the image of His

Son Yeshua by the Word and Spirit. But the god of this world is satan, and he wants to form man into his fallen image. God our Father wants to form us and preserve us whole in every part of our creation, spirit, soul, and body.

> **And the very God of peace sanctify you wholly; and [I pray God] your whole spirit and soul and body be preserved blameless unto the coming of our Lord Jesus Christ.**
> **1 Thessalonians 5:23 KJV**

But satan and his kingdom are masterful at hijacking and blinding our makeup, spirit, soul, and body to form us into broken people from the inside out.

THE "PAIN" OF A BROKEN HEART

I want to attempt to show you how spiritually and psychologically satan can break the human heart and thus form a broken person from the inside out.

The purpose of this insight is for the sake of discernment. We need to understand what the enemy is doing and what he is trying to pervert in creation to get it to bend to his will.

For the most part, a broken heart has its origins in social and relational separation. This separation usually comes in the form of reproaches and loss. Psalm 69:20 says just that.

Reproach hath broken my heart; and I am full of heaviness: and I looked [for some] to take pity, but [there was] none; and for comforters, but I found none.
Psalm 69:20 KJV

I will discuss in much more depth how reproaches and loss open the door to a broken heart in subsequent chapters, but it is important to know that now so we can begin to understand the pathway satan uses to form us into broken people.

The "Pain" Of A Broken Heart

We started this chapter by highlighting that humans will often use physical pain descriptors and phrases to describe what they are feeling when their heart is broken. They may say things such as, "That hurt", "It's just so painful", and the like. Even the Bible does this in Psalm 42 when trying to convey in words what the reproaches that came to them felt like.

[As] with a sword in my bones, mine enemies reproach me; while they say daily unto me, Where [is] thy God?
Psalm 42:10 KJV

Did you catch that? The psalmist is comparing the way these reproaches feel to a physical sword being thrust into their bones! That is quite a statement, but there is actually scientific truth to this.

I want to introduce a scientific phenomenon called "Pain Overlap". Pain overlap refers to the scientific observation that shows physical pain and social pain are processed on many of the same neural pathways. This is why when a person is rejected and reproached by another person, they might say, "That hurt!" Even though there is no physical pain present.

Now, to be transparent, the medical community technically calls this the "Pain Overlap Theory". However, the reason they added the word theory is that they are still not 100% sure which neural pathways social and physical pain share. Social and physical pain are certainly not processed in the exact same way in the brain, but there is an observational overlap shown by brain imaging. This is also clear from the well-known observations that physical pain can be alleviated by positive social encounters. Conversely, social pain can be relieved (false comfort, I may add) by painkillers like opioids. Why would one affect the other? Because they share neural pathways, experiences that bring relief to social pain also bring relief to physical pain and vice versa.

The "Pain" Of A Broken Heart

This understanding is going to begin to give us some insight into how satan can form a person to be broken. What I mean by 'broken' is a person who is formed and even begins to have their personality formed into someone who does not trust, avoids relationships, has their hopes deferred, and may even conclude by sending the brain into dysfunction, resulting in a diagnosable mental illness.

Now, really track with me here, and you will see the progression. Most medical professionals agree that the primary function of pain is to signal imminent or actual danger, promote avoidance of dangerous stimuli and threats, and aid in survival. The pain signal activates a small gland in your brain called the Dorsal Anterior Cingulate Cortex (dACC), which aids in our ability to focus and shift focus away from certain stimuli and onto other stimuli. When pain is present, this gland (the dACC) keeps a person's focus on the pain until a response to alleviate the pain is activated. A silly example to illustrate this would be getting your hand stuck in a mousetrap. The pain signal activates the dACC to stay focused on the pain the mousetrap is causing until you use your other hand to free yourself from the trap. If this were to happen to you, chances are you would not have a drawn-out thought process of what to do but would simply go into an alarm state, and without any rational thought, your other hand would come to aid in the survival of your hand that is stuck.

This is because the dACC activates the limbic system into an alarm state, also known as fight or flight. When this happens, the prefrontal cortex of the brain, which is responsible for rational decisions and foresight, becomes underactive, so the brain, and thus the person, goes into survival mode. This survival mode is going to cause the person to do whatever it takes to survive or stop the pain without regard to the long-term consequences of their actions.

The "Pain" Of A Broken Heart

One of the primary pain responses to alleviate and survive pain is avoidance, and for good reason when it comes to physical pain. A classic example, but a good one, is someone's hand touching a hot stove. Pain causes a person to remove their hand from the hot stove as quickly as possible and also teaches them to now AVOID touching a hot stove. The way God created us, we can be taught, or should I say formed, into avoiding things we equate with physical pain.

But if we are not aware of satan's devices, we may not realize that his kingdom will use this process to ensnare us. You see, if social and physical pain share some of the same neural pathways, then there is a similar type of processing that happens, and look how quickly and easily it can happen.

Let's say that a person is rejected and reproached in a relationship or suffers the loss of a relationship. Because the pain processing is similar, the dACC gland is activated to cause the person to focus on the cause of the pain. In this case, it is not physical pain but social pain. This is why people who have been reproached can't seem to think of anything else but the reproach. The dACC also triggers the limbic system into action and puts the brain into an alarm state that causes the person to go into survival mode. Now remember when a person is in survival mode the prefrontal cortex is underactive, which is responsible for making rational decisions that are good for the long-term well-being of a person, but the limbic system is only concerned with alleviating the pain as quickly as possible and surviving the pain experience and other pain experiences that may come in the future. Remember that the primary way to deal with the pain experience is avoidance.

It happens so quickly. When a person is rejected and reproached, it's "painful", therefore, the brain is processing in a way that causes the person to get away from the source of the pain and avoid it ongoing. **So, in social pain, the conclusion is** relationships cause pain, so avoid relationships, and people, and this even goes for avoiding God!

And just like that, a person has been formed into a broken person who now finds it difficult to trust God and others.

But now this person, in the name of "safety" and "avoidance" of pain, is transgressing the two great commandments to love the LORD your God with all your heart, all your soul, and all your mind and to love your neighbor as yourself.

> Master, which [is] the great commandment in the law? Jesus said unto him, Thou shalt love the Lord thy God with all thy heart, and with all thy soul, and with all thy mind. This is the first and great commandment. And the second [is] like unto it, Thou shalt love thy neighbour as thyself. On these two commandments hang all the law and the prophets.
> Matthew 22:36-40 KJV

This is also why forgiveness to those who have hurt you is so important. It seems to be the only way to stop the processing of social pain in this way.

To whom ye forgive any thing, I [forgive] also: for if I forgave any thing, to whom I forgave [it], for your sakes [forgave I it] in the person of Christ; Lest Satan should get an advantage of us: for we are not ignorant of his devices.
2 Corinthians 2:10-11 KJV

When someone has been reproached and is in the midst of processing, they become focused on the person that hurt them or the circumstance. A lot of times, people will teach someone who is focused on the issue they are in bitterness. I don't think it has turned to bitterness yet, but are simply processing and trying to make sense of the reproach, but that can be a trap too. We will never understand why satan influences so many people to hurt others, and they act it out in ignorance. The only way to stop this processing of social pain so that it does not conclude in avoiding relationships altogether is to forgive.

But if a person does not forgive, or does not know to forgive, but rather concludes relationships are painful, relationships involve people, and therefore people should be avoided, there will be long-term consequences that represent the curse, not the blessing.

Isolation and withdrawal can compound into depression, anxiety, lethargy, and seeking after false comforters, and can begin to bring on dysfunction in the physical body causing diseases and disorders.

What is tragic is that on the inside, a person like this who has been formed into being a broken-hearted person still wants fellowship because they were made for it. But satan has taught them it is not safe to fellowship, and now the person is double-minded and thus not stable. When a person is in this state, the limbic system continues to stay somewhat overactive and the prefrontal cortex underactive because people have been concluded to be a constant threat. The big problem with this is that in order for a person to apprehend love and a feeling of connectedness to God and others, the prefrontal cortex needs to be active and the limbic system at peace. This leaves a person with a greatly hindered ability to apprehend, feel, and receive love. Ultimately, this brings hope deferred regarding relationships, and it is my personal opinion that this is the torment of Post Traumatic Stress Disorder (PTSD).

The spirit of a man will sustain him in sickness,
But who can bear a broken spirit?
Proverbs 18:14 NKJV

What this verse is teaching us is that a person can, for the most part, endure physical infirmities, even physical pain, but no one can bear the pain of a broken spirit, and science agrees.

The "Pain" Of A Broken Heart

Look at these findings from an article published by the American Psychological Association titled, "Feeling Hurt: Revisiting the Relationship Between Social and Physical Pain"

Social and physical pain produce a different profile of psychological consequences. Results showed that social and physical pain both decrease overall needs satisfaction, and increase desire to aggress, negative effect, and feelings of being ignored and excluded. However, much like neural evidence of pain overlap, divergence is evident on closer inspection. Direct comparison has shown that physical and social pain triggered a different profile of responses along these measures: **Social pain was significantly more damaging than physical pain** *on overall fundamental needs satisfaction, sense of belonging, meaningful existence, and self-reported feelings of ostracism.*[1]

---

[1] Ferris, L. J., Jetten, J., Hornsey, M. J., & Bastian, B. (2019). Feeling Hurt: Revisiting the Relationship Between Social and Physical Pain. Review of General Psychology, 23(3), 320-335. https://doi.org/10.1177/1089268019857936

What is all this telling us? The Bible was true thousands of years before science ever could see or understand why, and it is still true today.

**The spirit of a man will sustain him in sickness,
But who can bear a broken spirit?
Proverbs 18:14 NKJV**

We are only beginning to scratch the surface of how deeply the broken heart affects mankind and how it is one of satan's most powerful weapons against humanity to attempt to bring them under his rule.

A WORD BEFORE WE KEEP MOVING AHEAD…

Now, to be clear, everyone's experience is different. For the sake of explanation, the examples and pathways I used were very straightforward and black and white. Brokenness is more like a spectrum than people fitting into a category of broken or whole. My hope and prayer is that God is able to use this type of insight, by the wisdom of the Holy Spirit, to show the reader individually how satan and his kingdom may have caused this type of damage and mindset in various areas of life and relationships.

Also, some of you may be eager to get to more solutions for the broken heart. Trust me, I like getting to solutions as fast as I can, but we need to take the time to gain understanding and discernment of what is going on within us and who our real battle is against. I will tell you that healing from a broken heart will involve repentance from many carnal solutions satan gives us along the way, lies, and then learning to walk in new ways such as putting your faith in what God says about you, not the enemy or others.

Ultimately, I see that the solution for the broken heart is trusting in the love and comfort of God, but as you will see in the coming chapters, we must recognize and remove the things in our lives that

The "Pain" Of A Broken Heart

hinder His love and comfort from healing our hearts.

You are doing great; let's keep going!

Chapter 5

Healing the Broken Heart from Reproach

HOW DO I BEGIN TO HEAL...

Now at this point, you might be saying, "David, I get it... I realize I have a broken heart, but now what? How do I begin healing?". Well, that depends...

When healthcare professionals are presented with a malfunctioning body part the first thing they want to do is find what is called the etiology of the symptom. The etiology simply means the root cause of the problem. Why do they want to find the etiology? Because that will often determine how they will treat the malfunctioning body part. There are numerous examples we could use, but let's say that an individual has been experiencing pain in one of their shoulders and it has begun to interfere with everyday activities in life. So, they go to an orthopedic specialist.

GOING TO THE RIGHT SOURCE OF HEALING...

Now let's stop right here and consider something. The individual did not go to a cancer doctor, an E.N.T. (ear, nose, and throat) doctor, or some other type of doctor to get their shoulder treated. When dealing with a broken heart and spirit we need to understand the type of help we need. We need spiritual help because a broken heart is a spiritual problem. A medical doctor may be able to relieve some physical systems stemming from a broken heart and a psychologist might be able to bring a little relief from a broken heart but neither are equipped in their professions to deal with the spiritual issues of man. But the Father, through Yeshua, has equipped the Body of Messiah with gifts by the Holy Spirit to help the Body bring healing to the Body.

Let's go back to one of our foundational passages of Scripture, Isaiah 61, and remember what is necessary for the Messiah to heal the brokenhearted.

The Spirit of the Lord GOD [is] upon me; because the LORD hath anointed me to preach good tidings unto the meek; he hath sent me to bind up the brokenhearted, to proclaim liberty to the captives, and the opening of the prison to [them that are] bound;
Isaiah 61:1 KJV

The only way for the Messiah and for us to do anything mentioned in Isaiah 61 that He and we are mandated to do is for us to be anointed with the Holy Spirit. Remember the broken heart and spirit is a spiritual issue caused by satan's kingdom and the only way to defeat the spiritual kingdom of darkness is with the more powerful Holy Spirit sent to establish the Kingdom of God. And the Holy Spirit has been given to the Body of Messiah to edify, profit, and heal the Body.

But speaking the truth in love, may grow up into him in all things, which is the head, [even] Christ: From whom the whole body fitly joined together and compacted by that which every joint supplieth, according to the effectual working in the measure of every part, maketh increase of the body unto the edifying of itself in love.
Ephesians 4:15-16 KJV

But the manifestation of the Spirit is given to each one for the profit [of all]: for to one is given the word of wisdom through the Spirit, to another the word of knowledge through the same Spirit, to another faith by the same Spirit, <u>to another gifts of healings by the same Spirit</u>, to another the working of miracles, to another prophecy, to another discerning of spirits, to another [different] kinds of tongues, to another the interpretation of tongues.
1 Corinthians 12:7-10 NKJV

Hopefully, it is now clear that we need to seek the right people and Spirit to find healing for the broken heart and spirit.

THE ORIGIN OF THE BROKEN HEART IS ESSENTIAL...

So back to my example of a malfunctioning, painful shoulder and why a healthcare professional would want to know the etiology of why it is malfunctioning and in pain. Pain in the shoulder could have its origins in several things. The pain could be caused by: a torn rotator cuff, a torn labrum, tendonitis, bone spurs, bursitis, arthritis, osteoarthritis, dislocation, pinched nerves, and sudden pain in the left shoulder could even be a heart attack. Now the reason a healthcare professional would want to know which of these issues is causing the shoulder pain is because each of these issues requires a different treatment plan for healing.

It's the same concept with the broken heart. The shoulder pain is shoulder pain and a broken heart is a broken heart but it is essential to understand what is causing the issue because that will determine the method of treatment or what issues of the heart must be addressed for healing to occur.

The Word of God is actually quite specific about what causes a broken heart and when we understand what causes a broken heart we can also look to the Word of God for the cure.

A DIAGNOSTIC QUESTION…

Now I want to go back to the original questions I asked in chapter 1 and focus on just one of them.

Were you wounded by the words and/or actions of another, and since then, feel insecure and have difficulty trusting God and others?

If you answered yes to this question let me say more than just your feelings were hurt, your heart was broken. Maybe you often find yourself feeling heavy and depressed. Perhaps it seems like you are all alone and you find it difficult to confide and trust others for support, advice, and encouragement. You simply don't feel yourself, but cannot seem to "snap out of it". Maybe you feel ensnared by these thoughts and feelings and only find a semblance of peace by withdrawing from others or engaging in some kind of addictive behavior.

In Psalm 69:20, King David while in his own grief and pain was able by the Spirit of God unfold for us an amazingly accurate understanding of the origin and the progression of a broken heart. Let's read.

Reproach has broken my heart, And I am full of heaviness; I looked [for someone] to take pity, but [there was] none; And for comforters, but I found none.
Psalm 69:20 NKJV

Healing a Broken Heart from Reproach

King David tells us exactly what broke his heart. It was reproach(s). You can read about the reproaches he encountered in the first 12 verses of Psalm 69, but let's quickly define a reproach since it is not a word that we use often in our modern vocabulary.

A reproach is any type of scorn, disgrace, false accusation, rejection, betrayal, abuse, or any other words and/or actions toward an individual that leaves them shameful. So a reproach can cause a broken heart.

Now, according to the Scripture above, what is the very next thing that happens after the heart has been broken? ***"And I am full of heaviness".*** Now we begin to see the psychological and physical realities of a broken heart begin to manifest. The Hebrew word used here for the phrase "full of heaviness" is the word "noosh" which literally means to be sick. This means our bodies can go into dysfunction from a broken heart. Even the medical community has identified something called Broken Heart Syndrome that may occur following stressful life events. The types of sicknesses coming from the broken heart also may include psychological dysfunction such as depression or anxiety.

I personally believe the psychological aspect was what King David was dealing with in this psalm. We see again in Isaiah 61:3 that the English word "heaviness" is mentioned. This time the Hebrew word is not "noosh", but "keh-heh" which means feeble, dim, and obscure. This type of heaviness is specific to affecting the mind, personality, and hope of an individual.

What is perhaps most interesting is that heaviness in Isaiah 61:3 is identified as a spirit, the Hebrew word being "ruach". Ruach in Hebrew is always identifying a being that cannot be seen with the physical eye but can influence physical creation. The Bible is identifying the source of the sickness and feebleness of mind and body as coming from a "spirit of heaviness".

> **To console those who mourn in Zion, To give them beauty for ashes, The oil of joy for mourning, The garment of praise for the <u>spirit of heaviness</u>; That they may be called trees of righteousness, The planting of the LORD, that He may be glorified."**
> **Isaiah 61:3 NKJV** *(underlined mine)*

Why is it important to point out that heaviness is the result of a spirit? Because it shows this is not simply an emotion and our battle is not with ourselves when it comes to symptoms of heaviness, but with satan's kingdom. Satan and his kingdom understand that when our heart/spirit is broken we are in a state that we have less rule over our spirit and when that happens his kingdom can begin to come into our lives.

> **Whoever [has] no rule over his own spirit [Is like] a city broken down, without walls.**
> **Proverbs 25:28 NKJV**

You see, when our heart is broken our ability to resist the temptations of a spirit of heaviness is greatly hindered. The spirit of heaviness can influence a person with heavy thoughts that remind them of the reproach thus keeping the pain in place, bitterness and self-hatred come, and it paints a very bleak picture of the future causing hopelessness. All of this activates the limbic system as we discussed in chapter 4 and the person is feeling the pain of not being whole. They may become despondent, fatigued, lack motivation, or anxious and nervous.

So what does a person do when they are in pain? They look for relief and comfort. Let's go back to what King David said in Psalm 69:20.

Reproach has broken my heart, And I am full of heaviness; I looked [for someone] to take pity, but [there was] none; And for comforters, but I found none.
Psalm 69:20 NKJV

So when King David was full of heaviness from satan's kingdom what was his response? He looked for someone to take pity on him and he looked for a comforter. Let me pause and say that pity is not a bad word. It is most often used in the context of self-pity, which is a dangerous counterfeit of genuine pity coming from another to support the one in pain or distress. Pity simply means to acknowledge another's suffering and be empathetic and merciful toward them.

The next thing King David sought was comfort from another. When one is in pain, they will seek comfort. You know comfort really is the key to healing the broken heart, but it is a specific kind of comfort. It is a comfort that only comes from faith in the truth of the word of God that brings relief to the lies and reproaches that caused pain. We will discuss that in greater detail later in this chapter.

For now, let's go back to Psalm 69:20. It says he sought someone to take pity and sought a comforter but found none. It is at this point in the progression of the broken heart that the enemy really wants to ensnare a person. This legitimate need for comfort opens the door for the enemy to bring all kinds of counterfeit comforters into our lives.

I call the things we turn to for comfort apart from God, *carnal solutions*. What are some of these carnal solutions that the enemy temps us with when we are looking for comfort? Here are just a few, this is by no means an exhaustive list: withdrawal and isolation, anger, substance abuse, fornication, adultery (this includes pornography), or other addictive patterns like excessive shopping, gambling, and the like. Another example of a carnal solution is idolatry and the occult. Today people are flocking to yoga, various new-age practices, and false religions in an attempt to find comfort and peace.

The real subtlety of the enemy in all of this is all these unrighteous carnal "solutions" bring a very temporary semblance of comfort, but always leave a void, even guilt, and once done leaves a person needing to go back for more "comfort" even though they don't want to. Doing something when you don't want to do it is called being a slave.

Do you not know that to whom you present yourselves slaves to obey, you are that one's slaves whom you obey, whether of sin [leading] to death, or of obedience [leading] to righteousness?
Romans 6:16 NKJV

So satan and his kingdom use reproaches to weaken the human spirit to bring in heaviness and pain that needs comforting and then offers carnal "solutions" that in the end ensnare us and satan in this area of our life has become our master. The broken heart is a wile of the enemy.

Now, besides becoming a slave to these carnal "solutions" that ultimately lead to death there are two more snares we can find ourselves in.

THE BROKEN HEART LEADING TO 3 SNARES...

1. The first snare is becoming a slave to satan's kingdom and his carnal "solutions".

2. Because we have become a slave to carnal "solutions" we are no longer in fellowship with the Holy Spirit and thus the Father and Yeshua are no longer our Lord and Master. Since only God is love, we are left with a greatly hindered ability to trust and thereby have difficulty giving and receiving love and feeling connected to God and others.

3. Lastly, because there is fear, lack of trust, and uncertainty there is a greatly hindered ability for the desires of the inner man to initiate the actions needed to fulfill those desires. This leaves a person double-minded and self-conflicted.

I hope you are beginning to see that a broken heart is far more than an emotional crisis. It is a strategy of satan and his kingdom to ensnare the hearts and minds of mankind both believers in Yeshua and non-believers alike.

WHERE DOES THE BROKEN HEART MOST OFTEN OCCUR?

To me, this is perhaps the most insidious part of satan's strategy. I have found that there are two primary places where satan wants to use reproaches from others to cause a broken heart and those two places are:

1. The biological family
2. The Body of Messiah

Why is this so devastating? Because these are the two primary institutions of community and fellowship in which we are to feel the safest. These two institutions were ordained by God Himself for humans to learn how to love, be loved, serve, be served, learn about Him, and flourish as God intended every human being to do at every stage of life. The biological family and the Body of Messiah are the two places where the most healing is able to occur and conversely where the most damage can be done.

I have dealt with literally thousands of people who had varying levels of a broken heart and without embellishing I can confidently say that 99% of those broken hearts occurred in one or both of these institutions.

A lot of reproaches we face in life may not affect us to the levels we have been discussing, but the Bible again affirms the difficulties we face when these reproaches come from one or both of these institutions.

Let's look at Psalm 55:12-14.

For [it was] not an enemy [that] reproached me; then I could have borne [it]: neither [was it] he that hated me [that] did magnify [himself] against me; then I would have hid myself from him: But [it was] thou, a man mine equal, my guide, and mine acquaintance. We took sweet counsel together, [and] walked unto the house of God in company.
Psalm 55:12-14 KJV

The most hurtful reproaches are when they come from someone that we care about, and have a relationship and fellowship with. In the family unit, this is husband to wife, parent to child, brother to brother, sister to sister, and on into extended family. Why do we think that satan is trying so hard to divide the Body of Messiah? Why do you think he is so busy trying to destroy the family unit? **To cause broken hearts**, because when he is able to do that he can control and influence the hearts and minds of humanity to do his will and keep them blinded from the liberty, peace, joy, and righteousness of the one and only Living God our Father and His Son Yeshua.

WHAT IF IT WASN'T ABOUT YOU?

Often one of the dynamics that occurs with a broken heart is becoming offended with the person who reproached them. But it doesn't stop there, someone with a broken heart will often begin to start taking everything other people say and do as a personal offense too. They may even become stuck on all that has befallen them and the world begins to revolve around them and how others fail them.

Healing a Broken Heart from Reproach

I don't know about you, but I have learned that I am the least joyful and peaceful when I am thinking about all the wrong that has been done to me. I am the most joyful, peaceful, content, and fulfilled when I am not thinking of myself but rather looking out for the needs of others. If you find yourself struggling with this type of thinking I want to offer you another lens to look at your situation through that may bring a lot of freedom and healing.

What if your broken heart was less about you being dealt a bad lot or the person that reproached you and more about being a tactic of satan's kingdom? A tactic to neutralize you so that you can do no damage to his kingdom and little good for the Kingdom of God? Would that change things for you? Would that begin to motivate you to stand up and not stay a victim when reproached?

I have great compassion for the brokenhearted and I myself have been the recipient of compassion when my heart was broken. We are called to comfort each other with the same comfort we have been comforted with.

> **Blessed [be] the God and Father of our Lord Jesus Christ, the Father of mercies and God of all comfort, who comforts us in all our tribulation, that we may be able to comfort those who are in any trouble, with the comfort with which we ourselves are comforted by God.**
> **2 Corinthians 1:3-4 NKJV**

But at some point for healing to begin each one of us must decide that because we understand what satan is trying to do we will not take it personally, but rather take personal responsibility and serve the Kingdom of God and not the lies of the enemy.

HOW CAN WE BEGIN TO HEAL FROM A BROKEN HEART CAUSED BY REPROACHES?

One of the first things an individual needs to do is let go of trying to figure out why the person reproached you. Chances are they don't even understand why they did it. When Yeshua was being crucified by the ones He came to save, which may have been the ultimate reproach, He said, "Father forgive them for they know not what they do"

Then Jesus said, "Father, forgive them, for they do not know what they do." And they divided His garments and cast lots.
Luke 23:34 NKJV

Reproaches are going to come, especially if we are believers and followers of Yeshua and His ways. No matter how spiritual we become, reproaches, in particular from family and the Body of Messiah will hurt, sting, pierce, and cause uncomfortable feelings and emotions. But we can't take the reproach in and believe it. If you do believe the reproach of another it will become your confusing reality. Why do I say a confusing reality? Because it will be their word vs. God's Word within you.

This is the battle! The battle for the Word of God and what He says about you to reign in your heart and mind. It is the will of God to heal your broken heart! We began this book with the Messianic mandate to heal the brokenhearted in Isaiah 61, but look at these other Scriptures.

The LORD [is] nigh unto them that are of a broken heart; and saveth such as be of a contrite spirit.
Psalm 34:18 KJV

The sacrifices of God [are] a broken spirit: a broken and a contrite heart, O God, thou wilt not despise.
Psalm 51:17 KJV

He healeth the broken in heart, and bindeth up their wounds.
Psalm 147:3 KJV

For thus saith the high and lofty One that inhabiteth eternity, whose name [is] Holy; I dwell in the high and holy [place], with him also [that is] of a contrite and humble spirit, to revive the spirit of the humble, and to revive the heart of the contrite ones.
Isaiah 57:15 KJV

These are just a few of the numerous Scriptures telling us that it is God's heart to heal our broken hearts from the damage the enemy has done through others to us. Even if you did something worthy to be reproached for, it is in the past. When we repent from the speech and action we were reproached for and put our faith in the sacrifice of Yeshua for the forgiveness of sins we are clean and above reproach.

And you, who once were alienated and enemies in your mind by wicked works, yet now He has reconciled in the body of His flesh through death,

Healing a Broken Heart from Reproach

**to present you holy, and blameless, and above reproach in His sight--
Colossians 1:21-22 NKJV**

We have to believe that God is the healer of our heart, not the breaker of it, and that He will heal us. But there are some conditions to be met in repentance and turning toward our Father in faith to heal our broken hearts.

STEPS TO HEALING THE BROKEN HEART
(If you need guidance in repentance and prayer I have included prayers to assist you on pages in the back of the book.)

1. FORGIVE THOSE WHO REPROACH YOU!

Yes, before we are able to move forward we must forgive those who have reproached us. This does not mean we should remain a doormat for reproaches and not establish boundaries with those who continually hurl them at us, but we must forgive. I think many people misunderstand what they are doing when they forgive. Forgiveness is not having a burst of love for somebody in your heart or a certain feeling toward them. I would encourage anyone to set feelings aside when working through forgiving someone because those feelings can trick a person into thinking they have or have not forgiven a person.

Something important to note is that forgiveness and reconciliation are not the same thing. Forgiveness can be done by the willingness of an individual without the relationship being reconciled back to fellowship. Reconciliation takes two individuals willing to do what it takes in forgiveness and change to restore fellowship and relationship. Reconciliation should be a desire when a person forgives, but many factors may cause it to not be possible to reconcile. For example, the person who needs to be forgiven is deceased, or the person who needs to be forgiven is simply not physically, mentally, or spiritually safe to have fellowship with because of being bound in habitual sin.

SO WHAT ARE WE DOING WHEN WE FORGIVE SOMEONE?

When we forgive someone, what we are doing is deciding to not repay, retaliate, or take justice into our own hands and punish the person who sinned against us. So are we throwing justice out the window? Certainly not, but I have come to realize that only God is righteous enough to repay and bring justice correctly. When we take justice into our own hands, the result is that we will end up sinning against the person. We are allowed to rebuke and confront those who sin against us, in particular our brothers and sisters in the LORD, but We must remember that vengeance belongs to God alone.

'You shall not hate your brother in your heart. You shall surely rebuke your neighbor, and not

bear sin because of him. 'You shall not take vengeance, nor bear any grudge against the children of your people, but you shall love your neighbor as yourself: I [am] the LORD.
Leviticus 19:17-18 NKJV

Repay no one evil for evil. Have regard for good things in the sight of all men. If it is possible, as much as depends on you, live peaceably with all men. Beloved, do not avenge yourselves, but [rather] give place to wrath; for it is written, "Vengeance [is] Mine, I will repay," says the Lord.
Romans 12:17-19 NKJV

Forgiving someone is really a wonderful thing because when we do, the burden of enacting justice and judgment is entrusted to God, rather than a burden carried by us. And that brings us to step number two which is to repent for any area we have not trusted God, but before we move ahead take a moment and tell our Father you want to be like His

Son Yeshua and forgive all manner of sins that specific people have done to you through reproaches. If you are not able to find it within yourself to want to forgive then ask our Father for a desire and willingness to forgive. Please don't move on to step two until you have prayed and done one of the two things above.

2. REPENT FOR NOT TRUSTING GOD

Now you might be asking, "How have I not been trusting God?" If we are continually dealing with a broken heart from reproaches, then it is an indication that we have trusted in what the reproach is communicating to us and about us more than what God has said to us and about us. In that way, we have put our trust in man and not God. The words of those who reproach us tear us down, but the Word of the Lord builds us up.

And now, brethren, I commend you to God, and to the word of his grace, which is able to build

you up, and to give you an inheritance among all them which are sanctified.
Acts 20:32 KJV

Perhaps somebody said something to reject you, but the Word of the Lord says

Blessed [be] the God and Father of our Lord Jesus Christ, who has blessed us with every spiritual blessing in the heavenly [places] in Christ, just as He chose us in Him before the foundation of the world, that we should be holy and without blame before Him in love, having predestined us to adoption as sons by Jesus Christ to Himself, according to the good pleasure of His will, to the praise of the glory of His grace, by which He made us accepted in the Beloved.
Ephesians 1:3-6 NKJV

Maybe a parent abandoned you or disowned you as a son or a daughter. The Bible says,

**When my father and my mother forsake me,
Then the LORD will take care of me.
Psalm 27:10 NKJV**

Speaking of care, many people believe that no one cares about them as a result of past reproaches. But…

**Therefore humble yourselves under the mighty hand of God, that He may exalt you in due time, casting all your care upon Him, for He cares for you.
1 Peter 5:6-7 NKJV**

Maybe someone told you that you will never amount to anything and have no future…

Therefore do not be ashamed of the testimony of our Lord, nor of me His prisoner, but share with me in the sufferings for the gospel according to the power of God, who has saved us and called [us] with a holy calling, not according to our

works, but according to His own purpose and grace which was given to us in Christ Jesus before time began,
2 Timothy 1:8-9 NKJV

Or maybe someone put down your looks or insinuated in some way you are defective.

I will praise You, for I am fearfully [and] wonderfully made; Marvelous are Your works, And [that] my soul knows very well.
Psalm 139:14 NKJV

And we could keep going and going and going. Listen, any reproach that could ever come your way, the Word of God is there to confront it and discern it as a lie from satan's kingdom. But we must trust His Word above the words and reproaches of others.

I remember when this need to repent for not trusting God and His Word hit hard for me. In the past, I always felt a little justified in not trusting God. I didn't see it as something that was affecting me too badly. I didn't see it as a serious sin and something to be repented of, but simply something to try harder at or grow in. That was until I read in the prophet Jeremiah what was happening when I wasn't trusting God and the fruit it was producing in my life.

> **Thus says the LORD: "Cursed [is] the man who trusts in man And makes flesh his strength, Whose heart departs from the LORD. For he shall be like a shrub in the desert, And shall not see when good comes, But shall inhabit the parched places in the wilderness, [In] a salt land [which is] not inhabited.**
> **Jeremiah 17:5-6 NKJV**

Did you happen to read what is happening when we put our trust in man and not others? Our heart is departing from the LORD! That got my attention quickly. But then look at the fruit… A parched, famished person, and many people who have a continual unresolved broken heart feel this way mentally and physically. When we don't trust the LORD above man our heart is departing from Him and I hope that moves us to repentance because look at the fruit of those who do trust in the LORD.

"Blessed [is] the man who trusts in the LORD, And whose hope is the LORD. For he shall be like a tree planted by the waters, Which spreads out its roots by the river, And will not fear when heat comes; But its leaf will be green, And will not be anxious in the year of drought, Nor will cease from yielding fruit.
Jeremiah 17:7-8 NKJV

So before we move on to step 3 take as long as you need to come to your Father and repent for trusting in man's words and reproaches above God's Word and His grace. Remember, when we repent what we are doing is turning from serving the ruler of one kingdom to the ruler, Yeshua and the Father, of the Kingdom of God. Repenting allows us to be proper citizens of the Kingdom of God and Yeshua paid a high price for us to be able to do it.

3. REPENT FOR THE CARNAL SOLUTIONS TURNED TO FOR COMFORT.

For this step I would encourage each person to make a specific list of people, things, or other spirits they turn to when they are trying to comfort the pain of a broken heart. Perhaps in response to reproaches, you withdraw and isolate, get defensive, lie and fabricate that you don't care, or go into feeling sorry for yourself (self-pity). Maybe you turn to addictive behaviors such as fornication, pornography, overeating, substance abuse, or excessive spending of money. Or some of you may have turned to the occult, whether it be yoga, hypnotism, the new age, or a false religion that does not exalt Yeshua as Lord and Savior as the Bible teaches.

Take some time, make a list, and repent. Remember, when we turn to these carnal solutions we have made them master in our life and they are not the ways of the Kingdom of God where true healing occurs.

> **Do you not know that to whom you present yourselves slaves to obey, you are that one's slaves whom you obey, whether of sin [leading] to death, or of obedience [leading] to righteousness?**
> **Romans 6:16 NKJV**

There are instances, in particular when a person has been serving these sins for a long period of time, that they may need deliverance from an evil spirit that has been allowed to oppress them because of long-term disobedience to God's Word knowingly or unknowingly. If you know a trusted brother or sister in the Lord that is able to help you with that, pray about reaching out to them. If you don't know anyone then tell those spirits yourself to go after repenting.

Now having done all this, place your faith and trust in God totally for your acceptance and your defense. Reproaches will surely come, but they don't have to break your heart ongoing. Each time a reproach comes, go to your Father in Yeshua's name rather than those carnal solutions, forgive those that reproached you, and turn to God's Word for the comfort and edification that establish the truth in your heart over the lies of the reproach.

If we do this, our hearts can never be broken long-term again from reproaches!

REPENTANCE AND PRAYER FROM THE REPROACHES OF OTHERS

Father, I come to you in the name of Yeshua. I thank you that by His death and resurrection, you have made a provision for me to come boldly before your throne of grace to find mercy and help in times of need.

Father, I repent of the doubt and unbelief towards You and Your Word that caused me to believe that the reproaches of others' words and actions towards me were the truth, instead of what Your Word says about me being the truth.

I repent for believing (make a list of the specific reproaches said about you that do not agree with what God says about you)

Father, I also repent for judging you as a Father based on the actions of others who were not following your Spirit. Especially the words and actions of my earthly father.

Father, these are lies that I have believed that I confess and bring into the light. I believe that if I confess my sins You are faithful and just to forgive me of my sins and to cleanse me from the lies and unrighteousness. That is what I am asking for now.

Healing a Broken Heart from Reproach

PRAYER FOR DELIVERANCE

Father, I know that in all of our speech and actions, we are either serving satan and his kingdom or Yeshua and the Kingdom of God.

Father, I recognize the speech and action I have already repented of was obedience to the kingdom of satan, and that by repenting I am turning to obedience toward Yeshua and the Kingdom of God. Father, I know that participation with satan's kingdom brings bondage in my life, but I am ready to walk in the liberty of Your Holy Spirit.

I believe based on Isaiah 61 and many other Scriptures that Yeshua came to set me free from the bondage of satan's kingdom by the power of the Holy Spirit.

So in the name of Yeshua, by the power of the Holy Spirit, I command all spirits that have been permitted in my life by disobedience to go right now. I have repented and no longer serve those ways in my life, but I serve the Living God and from this day forward take my stand in my place of acceptance in the Kingdom of God.

Healing a Broken Heart from Reproach

PRAYER FOR HEALING

Father, In Psalm 34:18 Your Word says that you are near to the brokenhearted. In Psalm 51:16-17 Your Word says that you don't desire sacrifice but a broken and contrite heart in which you will not despise. In Isaiah 57:15, Your Word says that you dwell with him that is of a humble and contrite spirit to revive the spirit of the contrite ones.

Father, I have found it hard to give you a broken heart, but in Proverbs 23:26, you simply ask for our heart no matter what condition it is in. Father, I give you my heart. I trust you to take care of it, comfort it, and heal it, because you care for me, comfort me, and want to heal me.

Father, I understand that healing from a broken heart may be a journey, but I commit to the journey and am so thankful to be able to take the journey.

And Father, as I am healed and healing, use me to help fulfill the Messianic mandate and help lead others to You so they may also be healed.

In Yeshua's name, Amen

Healing a Broken Heart from Reproach

Chapter 6

Healing the Broken
Heart from Loss

In the last chapter, we discussed the type of broken heart that comes from reproaches stemming from the words and actions of others. In particular, when those reproaches come from those that are closest to us. We addressed how to specifically heal that type of broken heart, and now we will identify and learn to heal from another type of broken heart, a broken heart coming from loss. Now, there will definitely be some overlap between the two, but there are some differences and that is why I have dedicated a chapter to each.

WHAT IS A LOSS?

It seems self-explanatory but to make sure we are on the same page a loss in our context is when an individual has been permanently separated from a love object. In most cases, this love object will be another human being, but it could entail other things such as the loss of a specific purpose, career, or function. For example, my mother of blessed memory loved working with children and she was really, really good at it. At one point she developed and started a Christian after school program that was very successful. After almost a decade of running this program and developing strong relationships with children, parents, and employees, new management came to the church that the program was affiliated with. My mother's afterschool program was not part of the vision for the new leaders and the program was shut down. To say my mother was heartbroken was an understatement. Her heart was eventually healed and she did continue in her calling and purpose in working with children, but never in an afterschool program again. It was a permanent loss.

When we lose a loved one to death, or lose some aspect of a relationship with a loved one due to degenerative diseases or ongoing, unrepentant sin, these also represent a type of permanent loss in our life here on earth.

WHAT IS OUR RESPONSE TO LOSS?

When we experience loss as humans, it is normal and healthy to experience grief. But we need to understand that there is "normal" grief and "abnormal" grief. When I say, "normal" grief I put it in quotations because I don't want to give the impression that any grief is easy or routine. I think the reason we experience this phenomenon called grief and all the sadness, confusion, and wonderment that comes with it is that we were never designed by God to experience it. Remember that when God made man in the garden there was no death and therefore the ability to process death and permanent loss was not a necessary function for life.

What I do mean by "normal" grief is that the grief is being processed, the person grieving is not separating from others but receiving support, their heart is finding comfort and hope through God, and with time the grief subsides and the person moves on with life. It does not mean they forget the love object or don't miss it, but they are able to move on with life in peace. "Abnormal" grief is when the grief is not being processed, an individual is not being comforted, begins isolating, begins to lose meaning in life, and the grief does not subside thus leaving the person hindered in being able to move on with life in joy and peace. It is this "abnormal" grief that leads to a broken heart that won't heal and this is where we can even see the development of psychological and biological maladies.

Loss is something that we all face in life. We have either faced it, are facing it, or will face it at some point in our journey. We may even go through tremendous grief and sorrow, but that does not mean our heart has to be broken without repair.

The prophets said that Yeshua himself was going to be a man familiar and acquainted with grief. Even to the point that He would bear our griefs and sorrows.

> **He is despised and rejected by men, A Man of sorrows and acquainted with grief. And we hid, as it were, [our] faces from Him; He was despised, and we did not esteem Him.**
> **Isaiah 53:3 NKJV**

In His time here on earth, the Bible records the times He grieved. There are numerous accounts, but perhaps the most well-known is His grief over the death of His friend Lazarus.

> **Therefore, when Jesus saw her weeping, and the Jews who came with her weeping, He groaned in the spirit and was troubled. And He said, "Where have you laid him?" They said to Him, "Lord, come and see." Jesus wept. Then the Jews said, "See how He loved him!"**
> **John 11:33-36 NKJV**

Paul also spoke of the grief of his brethren being separated from Messiah and the grief he would suffer if he lost certain people.

> **I tell the truth in Christ, I am not lying, my conscience also bearing me witness in the Holy Spirit, that I have great sorrow and continual grief in my heart.**
> **Romans 9:1-2 NKJV**

> **Yet I considered it necessary to send to you Epaphroditus, my brother, fellow worker, and fellow soldier, but your messenger and the one who ministered to my need; since he was longing for you all, and was distressed because you had heard that he was sick. For indeed he was sick almost unto death; but God had mercy on him, and not only on him but on me also, lest I should have sorrow upon sorrow.**
> **Philippians 2:25-27 NKJV**

I share these examples to help us realize that grief is not a sin, it does not mean you are weak, not spiritual, defective or any other sort of lie the enemy might want you to believe. But grief is a period of vulnerability in our lives and if we don't understand the wiles of satan and his kingdom he will exploit and try to use the loss he caused to break our hearts.

HOW CAN THE HEART BE BROKEN BY GRIEF AND LOSS?

I want to first begin with a diagnostic Scripture much like Psalm 69:20 for the broken heart coming out of reproaches. From here I really want you to track with me because from this Scripture and others, we can discern what hinders a grieving and broken heart from being comforted to a place where it is healed. The Scripture is Proverbs 15:13.

**A merry heart makes a cheerful countenance,
But by sorrow of the heart, the spirit is broken.
Proverbs 15:13 NKJV**

This Scripture is very straightforward in that it tells us exactly what is breaking the human heart/spirit. **It is the sorrow of the heart**. Knowing this, it makes logical sense that if the sorrow would be relieved and a merry heart returns then the heart is healed.

SO THE QUESTION IS, HOW IS SORROW ALLEVIATED?

Let's look to the Scriptures…

> **Remember the word to Your servant, Upon which You have caused me to hope. This [is] my comfort in my affliction, For Your word has given me life.**
> **Psalm 119:49-50 NKJV**

> **Blessed [be] the God and Father of our Lord Jesus Christ, the Father of mercies and God of all comfort, who comforts us in all our**

> **tribulation, that we may be able to comfort those who are in any trouble, with the comfort with which we ourselves are comforted by God.**
> **2 Corinthians 1:3-4 NKJV**

Let's also look at what is an antidote to mourning in the Messianic mandate Scripture we started with.

> **"The Spirit of the Lord GOD [is] upon Me, Because the LORD has anointed Me To preach good tidings to the poor; He has sent Me to heal the brokenhearted, To proclaim liberty to the captives, And the opening of the prison to [those who are] bound; To proclaim the acceptable year of the LORD, And the day of vengeance of our God; <u>To comfort all who mourn</u>, To console those who mourn in Zion, To give them beauty for ashes, The oil of joy for mourning, The garment of praise for the spirit of heaviness; That they may be called trees of righteousness, The planting of the LORD, that He may be glorified." Isaiah 61:1-3 NKJV** (*underlined mine*)

From these Scriptures, it is safe to conclude that what the heart needs during grief and sorrow is the comfort of God and His Word. What that means is if someone's sorrow, grief, or loss is comforted by the comfort of God then the broken heart would begin to heal and eventually completely heal. Sorrow that is comforted by God does not break the human heart and spirit as Proverbs 15:13 says that sorrow does. So there is a very basic distinction and that is there is sorrow that is comforted by God and there is the same type of sorrow, but it is a continual and perpetual sorrow that is not comforted by God. A wound left untreated becomes infected and causes many problems. Likewise, sorrow left uncomforted becoming continual sorrow causes many, many problems in one's life. What type of problems? Well, many of the same problems that come with a broken heart from the reproaches of others: depression, fatigue, lethargy, addictions, the occult, and relationship breakdown with others.

But the distinction between comforted sorrow by God and uncomforted sorrow leads us to a very fundamental question…

HOW CAN THERE BE UNCOMFORTED SORROW WHEN THE BIBLE IS FULL OF PROMISES TO COMFORT OUR SORROWS?

Does God pick and choose who He will comfort? No, as always the issues and hindrances lay with us not God, and we know this because in Him there is no inquiry, unrighteousness, or partiality.

To declare that the LORD is upright; [He is] my rock, and [there is] no unrighteousness in Him.
Psalm 92:15 NKJV

"Now therefore, let the fear of the LORD be upon you; take care and do [it], for [there is] no iniquity with the LORD our God, no partiality, nor taking of bribes."
2 Chronicles 19:7 NKJV

So it is not that God does not want to comfort our sorrows or that He is unwilling, but we become separated from Him and His comfort.

Now, before we move forward I want to implore you to guard your heart from guilt and condemnation. We want to shine a light on things that are wrong in a person's life not condemn them or shame them, but to show the person the problem in faith that they can be forgiven, healed, and restored.

HOW DO WE, EVEN AS BELIEVERS IN YESHUA BECOME SEPARATED FROM HIS COMFORT?

I believe Isaiah has some insight…

Behold, the LORD'S hand is not shortened, that it cannot save; neither his ear heavy, that it cannot hear: But your iniquities have separated

between you and your God, and your sins have hid [his] face from you, that he will not hear.
Isaiah 59:1-2 KJV

Iniquities in our life are able to separate us from God. Although there are many different ways to define iniquities, I tend to understand iniquity as ways and attitudes of the heart that we are not always aware of because they are the residue of our ancestors' disobedience to God in the generations before us.

So if an iniquity can separate us from God and as a result hinder us from experiencing Him comforting our sorrow, what is the iniquity that we need to identify? Perhaps if we could identify it and make a change through repentance then the comfort of God would flow into us as a work of the Holy Spirit and our broken hearts would be healed.

THE MOST COMMON INIQUITY THAT SEPARATES US FROM THE COMFORT OF GOD IS...

Many people say that Job is the best example in the Bible of how to suffer loss and go through grief. Well, the Bible does say that Job had patience and perseverance.

Indeed we count them blessed who endure. You have heard of the perseverance of Job and seen the end [intended by] the Lord--that the Lord is very compassionate and merciful.
James 5:11 NKJV

And to be fair I am not so sure I would have responded much differently in his situation. Perhaps even worse. I mean, the man suffered a great loss in losing his children and eventually his health, but I have come to find out that many people don't read the last ten chapters of Job because if they did, they would have realized that Job was being rebuked and corrected for his attitude and words in the first thirty-one chapters of the book of Job. However, it was a blessing for Job that this correction came because until he was shown the iniquity that separated him from the comfort of God in his affliction he stayed broken and was not getting better, but worse.

Beginning in chapter 32 of the book of Job enters a young man named Elihu, and in the next five chapters he shows Job the condition of his heart and the error of his three friends who were not able to help Job find the cause of his continual sorrow. Elihu also prepares the way for the LORD to speak to Job and bring final correction to repentance and full restoration in the last four chapters.

Obviously, you will need to go and read these chapters in their fullness on your own, but I want to highlight a few passages that will expose the iniquity Job was dealing with, and oftentimes we deal with concerning an unhealed broken heart stemming from a loss. Let's read carefully with an open heart to learn and be corrected ourselves.

> "Surely you have spoken in my hearing, And I have heard the sound of [your] words, [saying], 'I [am] pure, without transgression; I [am] innocent, and [there is] no iniquity in me. Yet He finds occasions against me, He counts me as His enemy; He puts my feet in the stocks, He watches all my paths.' "Look, [in] this you are not righteous. I will answer you, For God is greater than man.
> Job 33:8-12 NKJV

"For Job has said, 'I am righteous, But God has taken away my justice; Should I lie concerning my right? My wound [is] incurable, [though I am] without transgression.' What man [is] like Job, [Who] drinks scorn like water, Who goes in company with the workers of iniquity, And walks with wicked men? For he has said, 'It profits a man nothing That he should delight in

God.' "Therefore listen to me, you men of understanding: Far be it from God [to do] wickedness, And [from] the Almighty to [commit] iniquity.
Job 34:5-10 NKJV

'Job speaks without knowledge, His words [are] without wisdom.' Oh, that Job were tried to the utmost, Because [his] answers [are like] those of wicked men! For he adds rebellion to his sin; He claps [his hands] among us, And multiplies his words against God."
Job 34:35-37 NKJV

There is much, much more that is said but I believe these passages suffice to get the point across. In all of these passages of Scripture, Elihu is calling to record what Job himself said and corrected him. Some may be asking, "How do we know Elihu is right? Didn't Job's friends have to repent?" Yes, Job's three friends did have to repent, but Elihu is the fourth standing by and was never commanded to repent by the LORD. That means he spoke the truth!

So what is the truth that Elihu is bringing to light? That Job blamed God for his circumstances! He even went as far as to say in one of the passages we just read that God was his enemy!!!

When we blame God for a loss in our lives we have made Him the problem. Why is that an issue? Because if we have made God the problem then we will never trust Him in a way in which we can approach Him as the solution, and the solution is His comfort and love in our sorrow.

When a person faces loss, the enemy almost always brings a temptation to blame God for the loss rather than letting that person see satan and his kingdom are the ones responsible. Even in death, God did not originally intend for death to occur, but because satan rebelled against God, and sin entered mankind through disobedience and the wages of sin is death we need to blame satan for the death of our loved ones that we miss whether premature or at full age. If you have lost a loved one and are unsure of their salvation, that is not God's fault. It was satan blinding them from the truth and let me also say this... The LORD is a far more fair and merciful judge than any of us are and whatever He judges for a person's eternity is the absolute right thing. We have to come to this place of never questioning God's love, and integrity, and that He ALWAYS does what is right.

Another snare the enemy will try to lay is getting a person to blame themselves for the loss. This results in guilt and guilt will often manifest in blaming others, including God. Look at what Adam and Eve did when they felt the guilt of their sin.

And He said, "Who told you that you [were] naked? Have you eaten from the tree of which I commanded you that you should not eat?" ... And the LORD God said to the woman, "What

[is] this you have done?" The woman said, "The serpent deceived me, and I ate."
Genesis 3:11, 13 NKJV

Yes, there was truth in what they said but do you see what is missing? When confronted with a direct question about their actions, both Adam and Eve did not take responsibility and blamed someone else.

THE RESULTS OF BLAMING GOD

If we blame God for the loss we are saying that He is not righteous. In loss and pain, we must always remember and resist any temptations that would say God is not righteous, because if we believe that lie and make Him responsible for the loss and make Him unrighteous then we are easily separated from His constant, sufficient, and always available comfort and hope.

If we believe that God is not righteous in our loss then we will not be able to trust that He is trustworthy and safe. If we don't trust He is trustworthy and safe we will not open our hearts to Him in trust for Him to comfort our sorrows so that our hearts can be healed.

The result is this: A broken heart that will not heal because it cannot be comforted by God. This leaves a person fearful and stressed because now they only have themselves to look to. This will activate the limbic system and keep it activated and begin to affect the mind and body. With that said, I want to take a moment to discuss the connection between our heart and body.

A sound heart [is] life to the body
Proverbs 14:30a NKJV

THE HEART AND BODY CONNECTION

Here in Proverbs 14:30, the Bible communicates to us that there is a connection between the condition of our heart and our physical body. Even more amazing in this verse the Hebrew word translated as "sound" is the word "mar-pay" which literally means healed or cured. So Proverbs 14:30 could read, "A healed heart is life to the body". If it can be read like that then we can also understand it conversely as "an unhealed heart is death to the body".

Many people in the Body of Messiah today are seeking and crying out for healing from various diseases of the mind and body spanning numerous disease classes only to see their condition worsen over time. These are sincere people, people of faith, but they do not understand that until their hearts have been healed from the reproaches and losses of their past, physical healing may elude them. It is not uncommon for a person to begin to see physical healing and diseases begin to dissipate without any prayer or medical intervention when God their Father heals their broken heart. Remember, the result of a healed heart is not just joy and peace, but according to Proverbs 14:30, life to the body.

My aim in pointing this out is not to dig into the inner workings of physiology and show how the body is responding in dysfunction to the thoughts, feelings, and pain of a broken heart, but simply to show you there is a possible connection between your broken heart and any diseases you may be dealing with. I have seen numerous people healed of all kinds of diseases when their heart was healed, and in this chapter, I simply want to build your faith that as your broken heart is being healed, also have faith that when it is healed, any diseases you may be dealing with will be healed too.

If you deal with any of the following types of diseases or maladies, consider that behind it could be a broken heart, and trust God to heal those areas in your physical body as your heart is being healed.

Possible diseases from a broken heart: mental illness (non-injury related), addictive behavior, issues stemming from a compromised immune system such as allergies, autoimmune diseases, and cancer. Digestive issues and what the medical community calls psychosomatic diseases including hypertension, migraines, fibromyalgia, or chronic pain (non-injury related). This is by no means an exhaustive list, but with all of these diseases and maladies, there has been extensive scientific research to show the connection between stress, sadness, and how our body systems respond.

THREE STEPS TO HEALING FROM A BROKEN HEART FROM A LOSS

Many people want more extensive instructions and more steps but this is really simple, although it can be hard to come face to face with our words and actions against God. But believe me, He will forgive you.

1. Confess and tell God that He is righteous and repent for blaming Him in any way for the loss.

2. Repent of any attitudes or words of doubt that says God does not want to comfort you.

3. Spend time with God in His Word and in prayer.

A lot of people want a formula for healing and that includes healing the broken heart, but speaking honestly it simply does not work like that. If our broken hearts were caused by fellowshiping with lies from the enemy and meditating on them day and night, we must also fellowship with Truth and get acquainted with Him in fellowship. It's His presence, not a formula that heals. Truthfully, all I am trying to do in this book is restore your faith that

God does want to heal your broken heart, He can heal your broken heart, and to help you remove and expose barriers that interfere with that.

Before reading any more in this book go spend some quality time with your Father. Go outside, go for a walk, go into your prayer closet, or whatever you do. Leave the electronics behind, leave this book behind, and just take yourself and maybe a Bible, but begin to reconnect with your Father through His Son until you begin to apprehend His comfort and presence with you.

REPENTANCE AND PRAYER FROM LOSS

Father, I come to you in the name of Yeshua. I thank you that by His death and resurrection, you have made a provision for me to come boldly before your throne of grace to find mercy and help in times of need.

Father, You know the losses that I have incurred in my life. You know the timely and untimely losses. You have known my grief, seen my tears, and heard my cries.

However Father, I also recognize that I have been separated from your comfort and peace in these losses and also recognize that I have blamed You, myself, and the lost love object.

Father I repent for holding you responsible for any loss in my life. I confess that you are perfect and righteous and that you do no wrong. I also confess that any part I played in the loss, real or imagined, can be forgiven and I don't need to hold onto any guilt for the loss. I also forgive anyone that I have held responsible for the loss.

Father, these are lies that I have believed that I confess and bring into the light. I believe that if I confess my sins You are faithful and just to forgive me of my sins and to cleanse me from the lies and unrighteousness. That is what I am asking for now.

PRAYER FOR DELIVERANCE

Father, I know that in all of our speech and actions, we are either serving satan and his kingdom or Yeshua and the Kingdom of God.

Father, I recognize the speech and action I have already repented of was obedience to the kingdom of satan, and that by repenting I am turning to obedience toward Yeshua and the Kingdom of God. Father, I know that participation with satan's kingdom brings bondage in my life, but I am ready to walk in the liberty of Your Holy Spirit.

I believe based on Isaiah 61 and many other Scriptures that Yeshua came to set me free from the bondage of satan's kingdom by the power of the Holy Spirit.

So in the name of Yeshua, by the power of the Holy Spirit, I command all spirits that have been permitted in my life by disobedience to go right now. I have repented and no longer serve those ways in my life, but I serve the Living God and from this day forward take my stand in my place of acceptance in the Kingdom of God.

PRAYER FOR HEALING

Father, In Psalm 34:18 Your Word says that you are near to the brokenhearted. In Psalm 51:16-17 Your Word says that you don't desire sacrifice but a broken and contrite heart in which you will not despise. In Isaiah 57:15, Your Word says that you dwell with him that is of a humble and contrite spirit to revive the spirit of the contrite ones.

Father, I have found it hard to give you a broken heart, but in Proverbs 23:26, you simply ask for our heart no matter what condition it is in. Father, I give you my heart. I trust you to take care of it, comfort it, and heal it, because you care for me, comfort me, and want to heal me.

Father, I understand that healing from a broken heart may be a journey, but I commit to the journey and am so thankful to be able to take the journey.

And Father, as I am healed and healing, use me to help fulfill the Messianic mandate and help lead others to You so they may also be healed.

In Yeshua's name, Amen.

Closing Thoughts

As I wrap up this insight into healing from a broken heart I want to leave you with four things to consider along the way.

1. IT'S A JOURNEY

It is important to remember that healing from a broken heart is rarely instantaneous. Healing from a broken heart is often a journey that takes time. Even physical wounds once treated take time to fully heal. So be patient with yourself and the process. With each repentance, and each step toward trusting God and others you will bit by bit feel stronger and stronger.

2. GIVE OUT WHAT YOU HAVE RECEIVED

Yeshua said to give out what you have received.

Heal the sick, cleanse the lepers, raise the dead, cast out demons. Freely you have received, freely give.
Matthew 10:8 NKJV

This does not mean you need to go around and tell everyone how to heal from a broken heart, but when you see a need or someone downcast, comfort them with the same comfort you yourself were and are comforted with.

Blessed [be] the God and Father of our Lord Jesus Christ, the Father of mercies and God of all comfort, who comforts us in all our tribulation, that we may be able to comfort those who are in any trouble, with the comfort with which we ourselves are comforted by God.
2 Corinthians 1:3-4 NKJV

This will not only be a benefit to those who hear you but will continue to reinforce for yourself the truths that have made you free. Oh, and you need not wait till you are healed to do so. Helping others and looking at their needs may help you heal because you won't be stuck on your own brokenness, but relying on God to help you help others.

3. GET INTO COMMUNITY

If any of the reasons we incurred a broken heart stemmed from the words and actions of others, the healing of our heart can also be hastened by the right words and actions of others. Remember that one of the carnal solutions the enemy gives us when our heart is broken is withdrawal. But we were made for fellowship with God and others.

> **"Teacher, which [is] the great commandment in the law?" Jesus said to him, "'You shall love the LORD your God with all your heart, with all your soul, and with all your mind.' "This is [the] first and great commandment. "And [the] second [is] like it: 'You shall love your neighbor as yourself.' "On these two commandments hang all the Law and the Prophets.'"**
> **Matthew 22:36-40 NKJV**

If we withdraw then we are not walking in these two commands and healing from God will be difficult to find because we will not be walking in His ways and the way He designed us to live.

4. IT CAN HAPPEN AGAIN...

The heart can be broken, healed, and yet broken again. But here is the confidence I want to impart to you and it's really simple. The truth that healed your heart the first time, is the same truth that will heal your heart again. Things are going to happen, reproaches and losses will occur, but you never need to be afraid of being stuck with a broken heart ever again if you allow the truth of God's Word to penetrate your heart.

Shalom and Blessings

And now, brethren, I commend you to God, and to the word of his grace, which is able to build you up, and to give you an inheritance among all them which are sanctified.
Acts 20:32 KJV

Prayers

Included is a list of prayers for you to be able to refer back to as often as you may need.

The list of prayers included are:

1. Repentance and prayer from reproaches
2. Repentance and prayer from loss
3. Repentance from carnal devices
4. Prayer for healing
5. Prayer for deliverance

1. REPENTANCE AND PRAYER FROM THE REPROACHES OF OTHERS

Father, I come to you in the name of Yeshua. I thank you that by His death and resurrection, you have made a provision for me to come boldly before your throne of grace to find mercy and help in times of need.

Father, I repent of the doubt and unbelief towards You and Your Word that caused me to believe that the reproaches of others' words and actions towards me were the truth, instead of what Your Word says about me being the truth.

I repent for believing (make a list of the specific reproaches said about you that do not agree with what God says about you)

Father, I also repent for judging you as a Father based on the actions of others who were not following your Spirit. Especially the words and actions of my earthly father.

Father, these are lies that I have believed that I confess and bring into the light. I believe that if I confess my sins You are faithful and just to forgive me of my sins and to cleanse me from the lies and unrighteousness. That is what I am asking for now.

2. REPENTANCE AND PRAYER FROM LOSS

Father, I come to you in the name of Yeshua. I thank you that by His death and resurrection, you have made a provision for me to come boldly before your throne of grace to find mercy and help in times of need.

Father, You know the losses that I have incurred in my life. You know the timely and untimely losses. You have known my grief, seen my tears, and heard my cries.

However Father, I also recognize that I have been separated from your comfort and peace in these losses and also recognize that I have blamed You, myself, and the lost love object.

Father I repent for holding you responsible for any loss in my life. I confess that you are perfect and righteous and that you do no wrong. I also confess that any part I played in the loss, real or imagined, can be forgiven and I don't need to hold onto any guilt for the loss. I also forgive anyone that I have held responsible for the loss.

Father, these are lies that I have believed that I confess and bring into the light. I believe that if I confess my sins You are faithful and just to forgive me of my sins and to cleanse me from the lies and unrighteousness. That is what I am asking for now.

In Yeshua's name, Amen.

3. PRAYER OF REPENTANCE FOR CARNAL DEVICES

Father, I come to you in the name of Yeshua. I thank you that by His death and resurrection, you have made a provision for me to come boldly before your throne of grace to find mercy and help in times of need.

Father, I recognize and confess that when my heart was broken from the reproaches of others and losses I have incurred in my life I turned to carnal solutions to try and cope rather than turning to You for direction, hope, and comfort.

Father, I repent for: withdrawing from God and people for fear of being hurt again, holding anger and resentment in my heart to protect myself, slander and gossip, self-pity, turning to false comforters like: drugs, alcohol, food, fornication, adultery, excessive use of technology, and overworking. Father, I also repent for seeking direction, safety, and comfort in idolatry and occultism: new age, yoga, false religions, cults, fortune telling, and any other form of idolatry and occultism not mentioned here.

Father, these are lies that I have believed and served with my spirit and body. I confess them and bring them into the light. I believe that if I confess my sins You are faithful and just to forgive me of my sins and to cleanse me from the lies and unrighteousness. That is what I am asking for now.

4. PRAYER FOR DELIVERANCE

Father, I know that in all of our speech and actions, we are either serving satan and his kingdom or Yeshua and the Kingdom of God.

Father, I recognize the speech and action I have already repented of was obedience to the kingdom of satan, and that by repenting I am turning to obedience toward Yeshua and the Kingdom of God. Father, I know that participation with satan's kingdom brings bondage in my life, but I am ready to walk in the liberty of Your Holy Spirit.

I believe based on Isaiah 61 and many other Scriptures that Yeshua came to set me free from the bondage of satan's kingdom by the power of the Holy Spirit.

So in the name of Yeshua, by the power of the Holy Spirit, I command all spirits that have been permitted in my life by disobedience to go right now. I have repented and no longer serve those ways in my life, but I serve the Living God and from this day forward take my stand in my place of acceptance in the Kingdom of God.

5. PRAYER FOR HEALING

Father, In Psalm 34:18 Your Word says that you are near to the brokenhearted. In Psalm 51:16-17 Your Word says that you don't desire sacrifice but a broken and contrite heart in which you will not despise. In Isaiah 57:15, Your Word says that you dwell with him that is of a humble and contrite spirit to revive the spirit of the contrite ones.

Father, I have found it hard to give you a broken heart, but in Proverbs 23:26, you simply ask for our heart no matter what condition it is in. Father, I give you my heart. I trust you to take care of it, comfort it, and heal it, because you care for me, comfort me, and want to heal me.

Father, I understand that healing from a broken heart may be a journey, but I commit to the journey and am so thankful to be able to take the journey.

And Father, as I am healed and healing, use me to help fulfill the Messianic mandate and help lead others to You so they may also be healed.

In Yeshua's name, Amen

About the Author

David is the Messianic Rabbi at Congregation Ammudim and founder of Ammudim Teaching Ministries. He has served in numerous roles during his many years of ministry, but none has he enjoyed more than helping people grow closer to God by helping them understand the Bible. He has a way of taking some of the most complex and seemingly controversial truths of the Bible and breaking them down into a simple, understandable way. David is also a frequent speaker at Messianic conferences, congregations, and churches around North America.

Ammudim Teaching Ministries
Congregation Ammudim

Ammudim.org

Stay Connected

Here are more ways to connect with teachings and resources by David Levitt and Ammudim Teaching Ministries.

YouTube @DavidLevittAmmudim
YouTube @CongregationAmmudim
Facebook @Ammudim

Website @ Ammudim.org
Donate @ Ammudim.org/Partner

Join our email Newsletters @ Ammudim.org

If you have questions, need prayer, or would like to connect with us you can contact us at info@ammudim.org.